CREATING
A CLIMATE
FOR **POWER**
LEARNING

CREATING
A CLIMATE
FOR **POWER**
LEARNING

WHOLE PERSON ASSOCIATES
Duluth, Minnesota

Library of Congress Cataloging-in-Publication Data
    Creating a climate for power learning : 37 mind-stretching activities / Carolyn Chambers Clark.
    160 p. 23 cm.
    ISBN 1-57025-139-8
    1. Group relations training—Problems, exercises, etc. 2. Group games. I. Title.
    HM134.C573 1997
    302'.14—dc21   96-51246
                                                          CIP

Printed in the United States of America

10 9 8 7 6 5 4 3 2 1

WHOLE PERSON ASSOCIATES
210 West Michigan
Duluth, MN 55802-1908
800-247-6789

I am indebted to Susan DiFabio and Judith Ackerhalt, two educators with engaging teaching styles. We spent years together, discussing learning theories and approaches. They have generously shared their expertise and creativity with me, and for that, I am grateful.

TABLE OF CONTENTS

LEARNING CREATIVELY

ABOUT THE AUTHOR

Carolyn Chambers Clark, EdD, ARNP, has a masters degree in psychiatric/mental health nursing from Rutgers University and a doctorate in education from Teachers College, Columbia University. She has been a learning facilitator for clients and students and a training/learning consultant for universities, health care organizations, and corporations for thirty years. Carolyn is a nurse practitioner with an active clinical practice focused on wellness and mental health. Her philosophy—anybody can be taught anything and have fun learning—is a theme in her practice and in her many books and articles.

Carolyn Chambers Clark can be reached at:

Wellness Resources
3451 Central Avenue
St. Petersburg, FL 33713

Creating a Climate for Power Learning

INTRODUCTION

Welcome to the challenging world of teaching and learning. Creating a comfortable, fun, and growth-promoting learning environment is an ongoing challenge. Participants are more likely to remember content and respond positively to a learning experience if they had fun doing it.

Learners are unique in their life experiences, values, needs, and learning styles. *Creating a Climate for Power Learning* is designed to help both novice and seasoned trainers prepare participants with varied backgrounds and needs to learn effectively. A secondary goal is to give participants something they can take with them to future learning situations—a better understanding of the learning process and their personal learning style.

The activities in this volume focus on all aspects of learning preparation from understanding values and attitudes to developing cooperation and creativity. Most have been tried out and perfected with adult learners in many settings. Keep in mind that no single exercise will work in every learning situation. Likewise, if you lack confidence in an exercise, you probably will not be able to communicate enthusiasm about it to learners. For that reason, I suggest you carefully read through an exercise prior to using it, then try it out with a couple of colleagues, family members, or learners prior to using it in the targeted situation. This will enhance your confidence and facility with the exercise and will allow you to adapt it to your group and learning goals.

Keep notes on what you liked about an exercise and how you might want to change it next time. Ask participants for their help. A suggestion box might be the best way to get honest feedback.

Don't be discouraged if participants aren't as enthusiastic as you are about a particular exercise. It takes time to build trust and a comfort level so that everyone feels free to speak openly. Be patient with yourself and your groups.

Be sure to explain what's involved in every exercise. Give participants a chance to pass if they don't care to share their viewpoints. Merely knowing they don't have to participate will often propel them into speaking up. You can help this along by accepting participant comments without judgment. Have a "no putdown" rule. Fun is part of the process, but when participants break the rule, remind them of it. Be aware that putdowns usually come from feelings of insecurity. Critical people may need additional support or brief, private reminders about the group's rules.

It has taken me years of discussion with colleagues and trial-and-error learning to develop some of the methods presented in this volume. In the spirit of sharing, they are presented for your use.

I hope they will assist you in your preparation of a productive learning environment. Use the exercises to expand your vision of teaching and learning, to bring your training sessions alive, and to create the spark of learning in all seekers of knowledge—including you!

Carolyn Chambers Clark
November 1996

ENERGIZERS

Present these exercises at any time during a training experience to energize participants, provide a needed break, encourage interaction, and enhance learning.

FILL UP YOUR ENERGY POOL— BREATHE!

This simple exercise shows participants the effect of breathing on learning.

GOALS
To try different ways to breathe.
To observe and understand the effect of breathing on learning.
To work with a partner to devise a breathing reminder cue.

GROUP SIZE
Unlimited.

TIME
15–30 minutes.

MATERIALS
Blank paper; pens or pencils.

PROCESS
▦ Introduce the topic of the exercise, then distribute paper to

participants. Ask them to rate themselves on a scale from 1–10 with 1 being bored, distracted, and stressed out and 10 being calm, energized, and ready to learn.

▓ Give the following instruction to participants:

▲ I am going to read aloud a number. Listen carefully to the number and attempt to remember it but do not write it down until I tell you to.

▓ Read the following number aloud: 1 5 2 4 3 6 5 9 2 1 3 4. After waiting 5 seconds, ask participants to write down as much of the 12-digit number as they can remember and to note any difficulties encountered in remembering it.

▓ Invite participants to pay attention to, but not change, their own breathing as they jot down answers to the following questions:

▲ Are you breathing through your mouth or your nose?

▲ Is your chest, your rib cage, or your abdomen expanding?

▲ Are you breathing rapidly or slowly?

▓ Tell participants that you would like them to focus on their breathing, then read the following script to the group, slowly and softly, pausing after each phrase:

Close your eyes . . .
Let your breath gently move to your abdominal area . . .
the center of your body . . .
Inhale energy and relaxation . . . feeling calm . . .
feeling comforted . . .
Continue to breathe effortlessly . . . calmly . . . peacefully . . .
exhaling easily whatever it's time to let go of . . .

After 1 minute, ask everyone to open their eyes, but to keep breathing slowly and from their center. Explain to the group that you are going to recite a second number. Ask them to listen closely and, while remaining relaxed, to attempt to remember it. Read aloud the following number: 5 6 9 0 3 1 4 3 3 6 8 9.

After waiting 5 seconds, provide the following instructions to the group:

⬥ Write down the number I just read aloud, remembering as much of it as possible.

⬥ Rate yourselves a second time on a scale from 1 (bored, distracted, stressed out) to 10 (calm, energized, ready to learn).

When everyone has finished writing, ask participants to share the results of this exercise.

Be prepared to deal with inconclusive or contradictory results.

Encourage participants to share their findings, extracting principles of breathing and learning. Conclude the exercise with the following comments:

⬥ Shallow, upper chest breathing reduces the oxygen available to your brain.

⬥ Centered breathing enhances circulation and gets more oxygen to your cells, including your brain cells. Centered breathing enhances learning.

VARIATIONS

Ask each participant to select a partner. Ask them to decide how each of them will use what they learned in this exercise about breathing and its effect on learning. Offer this suggestion:

Ask participants to select a partner, then to devise a way to remind their partner about using centered breathing at all times during today's learning experience.

Experiment with shallow, chest breathing and centered, abdominal breathing, using different measures of learning, such as memorizing a nonsense poem or jingle or doing a physical activity.

GROUP BACK RUB

*In this simple experiment, participants use the
soothing power of touch to energize each other.
This will promote group togetherness.*

GOALS

To examine the effect of touch on attitudes toward learning.
To give and receive touch as a warm-up and energizing experience.

GROUP SIZE

Unlimited.

TIME

10–20 minutes.

MATERIALS

Whistle; a carpeted or clean floor.

PROCESS

▦ Ask participants to rate themselves on a scale from 1–10 with
1 being bored, distracted, or stressed out and 10 being calm,

energized, and ready to learn. Instruct them to record that number so they can easily find it later.

Introduce the exercise with the following comments:

- Physical, mental, and emotional stress can lead to tension in the muscles of the neck and shoulders.

- Tense muscles contract and cut off the flow of blood to the tissues. When that happens, cells throughout the body do not receive adequate nutrition and oxygen. Because brain cells suffer from lack of oxygen, learning is impeded and attention is decreased.

- One key to good health and to creating a receptive environment for learning is to keep the blood flowing at an even pace throughout the body. Even if you aren't under great stress, sitting or standing in one position too long causes the blood to stagnate and restricts the energy flow. Touch can open up the circulation and energy flow again.

- Massage techniques range from simple to complex. The key to a rejuvenating massage is to first consult with your client to see what feels good to them. This will enable you to determine how much pressure to use during the massage. Most people have a preference as to the type of touch they enjoy during a massage—stroking, patting, squeezing, soft pounding, kneading, rubbing, lifting, etc.

- Touch is a universal antidote for stress. When administered with care, it can be a soothing bridge to friendship and camaraderie.

Ask group members to form a circle and sit down. Provide the following instructions:

Creating a Climate for Power Learning

- Today you are going to give and receive a back rub as a way to energize yourself.

- At this time, I would like every other person in the circle to give a back rub to the person to the right of them. Begin your back rub by using a variety of techniques on your partner. Listen to their response and vary your techniques, using the ones that are most pleasant to them. You will have 5 minutes to give this massage.

After 5 minutes are up, signal participants to switch roles.

- Now I would like all of you who were giving a back rub to sit back and relax as the person to the right of you in the circle gives you a soothing back rub. I will tell you when 5 minutes are up.

After everyone has had an opportunity to give and receive a massage, ask them to reevaluate themselves on a scale from 1 (bored, distracted, stressed out) to 10 (calm, energized, ready to learn).

After everyone has recorded their second rating, ask the group to compare their pre- and post-massage ratings. Encourage them to share any additional comments or insights they gained during this activity.

Conclude the exercise by leading a discussion on how back rubs might be used to reduce tension at other times in our everyday lives.

VARIATION

Explain to participants the benefits of self-massage. Instruct group members in this process by giving the following instructions:

- Begin the massage by wrapping your arms around yourself and giving yourself a big hug.

- Shrug your shoulders up and down.

- Make small then large circles with your arms.

- Rotate your ankles clockwise, then counterclockwise.

- Gently pummel your back and knead your shoulders.

- If you feel like it, slip off your shoes and gently knead your toes, feet, ankles, and calves.

HEEL, TOE, STOMP, STOMP!

Participants enhance their circulation, bring oxygen to their brain cells, and express their creativity using line dancing.

GOALS
To experience the fun of line dancing.
To reflect on their level of energy and enthusiasm after dancing.

GROUP SIZE
Unlimited.

TIME
10–15 minutes.

MATERIALS
A large room with enough room for line dancing; **Heel, Toe, Stomp, Stomp!** handout (optional); cassette player and country western tape containing a medium-fast song; paper Stetson hats or spurs are optional.

> *Practice the steps to **Heel, Toe, Stomp, Stomp!** prior to teaching participants.*

PROCESS

■ Introduce the goals of the exercise to participants and provide the following comments:

▲ Line dancing is a great way to include exercise in your life and to have fun at the same time. Don't worry if you miss a step or turn the wrong way.

▲ Giggles, laughter, and yahoos are encouraged. Ham it up, have fun, move your hips, shoulders, arms, and feet for a full body workout. Don't forget to stomp hard! It's a great tension reliever.

■ Ask participants to help clear away any tables or chairs to make room for the dance sequence. Instruct everyone to form one or more lines facing you.

■ Before turning on the music, demonstrate the dance steps to the participants. Ask them to copy your movements. Add one step at a time until the group has learned the whole dance sequence. When everyone feels ready, turn on the music and run through the sequence one or two times with the music.

■ Ask everyone to return to their seats and lead a closing discussion using the following questions:

▲ Do you feel more energy after dancing? Why?

▲ Do you feel more or less ready to learn?

▲ How could enjoyable group exercise improve your daily life?

*At this time, distribute the **Heel, Toe, Stomp, Stomp!** handout for participants to take home and practice the dance sequence at their leisure.*

HEEL, TOE, STOMP, STOMP!

Stand with your feet pointing straight ahead.

Two right toe fans: Sweep your right foot to the right, pointing your toe to the right, then return. Repeat once.

Right heel and toe taps: Tap your right heel twice in front, then tap your right toes twice in back.

Left foot stomp: Step on your right foot, heel first; shift your weight and stomp twice with your left foot.

Left heel and toe taps: Tap your left heel twice in front, then tap your left toes twice in back.

Right foot stomp: Step on your left foot, heel first; shift your weight and stomp twice with your right foot.

Vine right: Step to the right with your right foot. Step to the right with your left foot, crossing your left foot behind your right. Repeat these two steps, this time crossing your left foot in front of your right. As you bring your right foot to the front, scuff it along the floor, kick to the front, finish with your feet together.

Vine left: Repeat vine only to the left. While scuffing, make a half turn to the right so you are facing the back of the room. Vine right and then left again. At end of last vine, instead of scuffing, stomp your left foot once.

Repeat the dance.

©1997 Carolyn Chambers Clark Whole Person Associates • 210 West Michigan • Duluth, MN 55802 • (800) 247-6789

SOOTHE THE SAVAGE BEAST

Participants use sound and music to energize and calm themselves and to stimulate creativity.

GOALS

To explore the use of sound and music to energize.
To use music and sound to transmit learning information.

GROUP SIZE

Unlimited. For 20 or more, form groups of 6–8 participants.

TIME

10–15 minutes.

MATERIALS

Cassette player and an assortment of audiotapes containing music or sounds such as jungle noises, running water, ocean waves, etc. Choose a variety to soothe, stimulate, or energize.

PROCESS

▤ Introduce the exercise by asking participants how music affects their mood, their energy level, and their sense of creativity. Let participants vote on the type of music or sounds they want to listen to by raising their hands and voting as samples from each tape are played aloud. If there is a close vote, plan to play segments from two or three tapes.

Once the choice of music or sound is made, begin playing the audiotape and give participants the following directions:

  ▲ Find a comfortable sitting position in your chair.

  ▲ Close your eyes and picture whatever images are brought forth by the music. These images may be soothing like the rhythmic rolling of ocean waves, or they may be very stimulating such as wild animals chasing each other in a jungle setting. Let your mind wander and don't try to force any specific images. Allow your imagination to take control.

After 5 minutes, ask participants to open their eyes. Lead a closing discussion by encouraging them to share any images and feelings they had while listening to the music or sounds.

VARIATIONS

Distribute blank paper to participants and ask them to draw with their nondominant hand while listening to the music. (Drawing with your left hand when right-handed and vice versa taps into creativity.)

Ask the group to write, in a free-association style, without censoring what is written. Ask participants to use their nondominant hand which frees them from the constraints of the logical, left brain.

WHISTLE DIXIE

Participants find new energy as they
experience how whistling combines elements
of breath control, movement, and humor.

GOALS
To observe the effect that whistling has on stress, boredom, and distraction.
To take a break and reenergize.

GROUP SIZE
Unlimited.

TIME
10–20 minutes.

MATERIALS
None.

PROCESS
▪ Introduce the goals of the exercise, then ask participants to

whistle "Dixie" in unison. Giggles, chortles, and guffaws are encouraged.

- After whistling "Dixie," ask participants to whistle their favorite song either individually or while other members of the group are each whistling a favorite song.

- After the second round of whistling, ask participants the following questions:

  - What effect did whistling have on your energy level?

  - Was there a noticeable difference in how you felt before you began whistling and after you were finished?

  - Did you notice yourself feeling more energized or more tired?

- Lead a closing discussion by asking the group what is energizing about whistling. Encourage participants to offer ideas for other energizing activities.

VARIATION

- Form small groups of four participants and give the following instructions:

  - Decide as a group on a well known song to use as the theme song for our learning experience.

  - Select one participant to whistle the song, a second one to play the table like a bongo drum, a third one to pantomime strumming a guitar while vocalizing the song, and a fourth one to strike two metal objects together in time to the others.

  - If no one volunteers for the four parts, have the group write down the word "whistle" on one piece of paper, "bongo drums" on another, "guitar" on a third, and "metal percussion" on the last one. Have the group members draw which instrument they will play.

▲ When everyone is ready, ask each group to perform their song for the rest of the groups. Encourage yahoos, giggles, and applause.

Creating a Climate for Power Learning

HULA-KALULA

Participants learn that the hula and other forms of individual body movement can loosen stiff muscles, enhance circulation, and energize.

GOALS

To use movement to relieve tension, energize, and provide humor. To consider how vigorous movement can enhance health.

GROUP SIZE

Unlimited.

TIME

5–20 minutes.

MATERIALS

Hawaiian music on audiocassette; cassette player; (flower leis or grass skirts are optional).

PROCESS

▢ Introduce the benefits of movement and exercise, including some or all of the following points:

- Movement and exercise can open up blocks to circulation that result from sitting or standing in one position for a long period of time.

- Movement and exercise enhances production of the body's own feel-good substances, called endorphins, that raise mood and enhance self-esteem.

- Unfamiliar movements, like the hula, add to our enjoyment by tapping into our sense of humor and whimsey.

Provide the following instructions to participants:

- At this time, I would like everyone to stand up and stretch.

- When I turn the music on, begin to sway to its rhythm, and gradually use your hands and hips to tell a story.

After several minutes, request braver souls to volunteer to dance their hula in front of the group. Challenge participants to guess what story the volunteer is telling with their hula.

Conclude the exercise by leading a discussion on the benefits of movement to our overall health.

CREATING A
LEARNING PLACE

Set the stage for learning, enhance the learning environment, and empower participants to cooperate and
collaborate.

OUR LEARNING PLAYGROUND

*Participants use crayons, paints, sheets of newsprint,
props, and music to create a playground for learning.*

GOALS

To encourage participants to tap into their own creativity by using
various media to design a playground for learning.
To allow participants to experience learning from a different environmental perspective.

GROUP SIZE

Limited by wall space. A 10- to 12-foot wall hung with large sheets
of newsprint will be required for each group of 6–8 participants.

TIME

30–50 minutes.

MATERIALS

A playground backdrop will be designed on newsprint to hang up
along a wall, so sufficient quantities of the following materials
should be provided: plastic dropcloths to protect the wall and
floor; newsprint; watercolors, brushes, or colored marking pens;

masking tape; paper or plastic aprons to protect participants' clothing.

An assortment of other materials will be needed. You may ask participants to bring these articles or supply them yourself. Play materials: basketball, baseball, tennis racket, marbles etc.; an assortment of hats: baseball, western, football, sailor, etc.; a variety of music on cassette or CD; cassette or CD player; 3 x 5 inch cards with the painting and scene design assignments already written on them (e.g., paint a basketball hoop, paint a swing set, paint a slide, paint a hopscotch game, etc.); whistle.

> *Prior to the workshop, tape newsprint to the walls, backed by plastic dropcloths (if needed), and distribute other materials to each playground site.*

PROCESS

Set the stage for this enjoyable exercise with an energetic and humorous introduction.

- Today we're going to play, but first we must build a playground. When the play space is ready, you'll use it to learn a new skill.

- Have as much fun and use as much creativity as possible.

- No loud roughhousing is allowed and be sure to share with your neighbors.

- Stop whatever you're doing when the whistle is blown.

Form groups of six to eight participants; distribute assignment cards; provide the following instructions:

- Working together your group is going to paint a playground backdrop on the newsprint.

⊿ On the card you were given, you will find the piece of playground equipment you should paint. You will have 10 minutes to complete this part of the project. I will blow the whistle to signal when time is up.

▪ When the backdrop is complete, ask each person to select a hat and place it on their head. If participants bring their own hats, they can wear those. When everyone is dressed to play, explain to participants that they will have 5 minutes to learn a new skill, such as dribbling, pitching, or rope skipping, as they play at the playground.

▪ After 5 minutes, blow the whistle and reconvene the entire group. Ask the following questions to generate discussion:

⊿ How was your mood affected while you were creating the playground? Were you excited? bored? anxious?

⊿ How did the fun of developing the playground affect your learning of a new skill?

⊿ How could you use this technique to help you learn other new skills?

▪ Conclude the exercise by asking participants to share any additional comments they gained during this activity.

VARIATIONS

▪ Ask participants to keep their hats on and bring their toys or sporting equipment with them to the next learning segments. Ask them to speak from the perspective of their hat and equipment and later to report to the entire group on how this role affected their perspective, questions, and behavior.

▪ Use posters or a prepared playground background, saving participants' time and eliminating the need for paints and brushes.

Creating a Climate for Power Learning

■ Have newsprint in place when participants arrive. Ask them to paste or tape up pictures of basketball hoops, slides, swing sets, etc.

RITUAL FOR LEARNING

Participants learn the importance of rituals and how to create a ritual to fit the mood and needs of the moment.

GOALS

To open the self to trust and to play.
To bond with other participants.

GROUP SIZE

Unlimited.

TIME

10–60 minutes. An ongoing group might spend 10–15 minutes at the beginning of several sessions to plan, produce, and use the ritual.

MATERIALS

From the lists that follow, select the materials you will need for your workshop. Candles—scented or unscented, colored or white. (Make choices depending on group input or learning goals. For example, purple is a healing color, red and yellow are stimulating, blue is cool and soothing, violet is relaxing, and green is calming. Likewise lavender is a nerve tonic, geranium is reviving, and camomile is stimulating.)

Learning banner—a long length of fabric, the color and size to be determined by the group; other pieces of fabric; fringes or other decorative materials; glue.

Learning ribbons—lengths of wide ribbon in several colors; trimmings; scissors; glue; pins.

PROCESS

Introduce the session to the group and suggest that a ritual or ceremony is a good way to join the group together in their journey toward common learning goals. Bring to the group one or more of the following ideas:

> Unlike our Eastern brothers and sisters, Westerners are not accustomed to rituals or ceremonies as part of their learning experiences.

> Ceremony and ritual can indelibly etch a learning experience into our minds and souls. Such practices may seem awkward or strange at first, but they create a wholeness of mind/body/ spirit and a communion of souls for learning. At the very least, lighting a candle and meditating together for 5 minutes allows the group to be together, yet separate, in a moment of silence, sinking into the calm of a quiet place inside. It allows competition and a desire for the product of learning to flow away. The essence of learning, the process, then floats to the surface, continually unfolding and revealing itself from out of darkness.

Ask the group to choose a ritual or ceremony they want to focus on from the following list of suggestions:

- A special dance for hands or feet created by the group

- A song composed and then sung by the group

- A banner with words, symbols, or phrases of significance to the group on it

- A ribbon for each participant, to be designed, made, and worn during the training session

- A prayer or meditation to be said at the beginning and end of the training session

- A poem composed by the group and read at the beginning or end of the training session

- A cave painting of unique hieroglyphics or symbols the group wants to leave for posterity

- After the group has selected a ritual or ceremony, allow a few minutes for them to select the necessary materials or to determine what the materials will be and how they will be obtained.

- Allow 10–30 minutes (depending on the activity selected) for the group to create their ritual or ceremony. Wander among participants and offer suggestions if they need encouragement.

- When the group has finished devising the ritual or ceremony, allow time for them to try it out.

- When 10 minutes are up, reconvene the group and ask participants the following questions:

  - What did you learn about yourself by creating the ritual or ceremony?

  - What did you learn about the group by creating and using the ritual or ceremony?

▲ What memories were reawakened in you by creating the ritual or ceremony?

▲ If you encountered any problems during the process, how did you solve them?

▲ How could we use the ritual or ceremony created in the learning group in our training group? in our own lives?

ONE LEARNING PLACE

In this easy imagery exercise, participants use creative visualization to develop and then immerse themselves in an ideal learning environment.

GOALS
To explore the use of imagery as a way to create an ideal learning environment.
To practice an effective technique that encourages creativity.

GROUP SIZE
Unlimited.

TIME
20–30 minutes.

MATERIALS
Audiotape with relaxing music and cassette player; pictures or images to stimulate creative visualization; comfortable chairs, floor mats, or carpeting.

PROCESS

▦ Introduce the exercise to participants with a chalktalk on creative visualization.

  ▲ Creative visualization is the process of using internal images to heal, problem-solve, relax, or enhance learning.

  ▲ The mind does not differentiate between the images it creates and external reality. So, by creating positive images, we can overcome negative thought processes, which can disable us by creating anxiety, anger, depression, even physical illness.

  ▲ By learning to use creative visualization, we can enhance the learning process and embellish it with creativity.

  ▲ The ability to visualize is a learned skill and requires practice. As children, we were able to create images easily, but in school, logical process is valued and our imagery skills often get rusty.

  ▲ This exercise provides an opportunity for polishing our imagery skills and learning to use them to enhance learning.

▦ Ask participants to find a comfortable position while you put on a relaxing music tape. They may choose to sit in a chair or lie on the floor. Select a few pictures of pleasant buildings in peaceful surroundings and place them where everyone can see them.

▦ After allowing participants to look at the pictures for several minutes, read aloud the following script slowly, pausing after each phrase:

Close your eyes . . .
Gradually let your breathing move lower in your body
toward your center, your abdominal area . . .

Feel the sensation of your feet against the floor . . .
your back against the chair . . .
or your body against the floor . . .

Let an image come before you
of your ideal learning environment . . .
maybe somewhat like one of the pictures I showed you . . .
or different . . .
whatever has meaning for you . . .

Walk up the walk to One Learning Place . . .
Smell the smells associated with your ideal
learning environment . . .
hear the sounds . . .
feel the sensations . . .
see whatever there is to see in your ideal learning environment,
One Learning Place . . .

You are directing a video tour . . .
Let your camera zoom in on One Learning Place . . .
See even the tiniest details about it . . .
Drink in the wonder and awe of being in your favorite
learning place . . .

If there are other people there, pay attention to what
they are doing . . .

Look at yourself inside One Learning Place . . .
How are you acting? . . .
How are you feeling? . . .
What are you thinking about? . . .

Now expand your vision . . .

What do you see happening? . . .
What do you hear? . . .

How do you feel about being at One Learning Place,
your ideal place for learning? . . .
Be sure to take a reading of your body and mind . . .

Take a few minutes now to really immerse yourself
inside One Learning Place . . .
allowing yourself to soak up all the wonderful things
happening there . . .
Let them flow over you as a color, a soothing liquid, or in some
other form that has meaning for you . . .

Enjoy! . . .
Have a wonderful learning experience . . .
I'll let you know when it's time to return . . .

Allow the group to go on a silent journey in their creative visualization for the next 2–5 minutes. After the time has elapsed, continue reading the script slowly, pausing after each phrase:

You are finishing your journey to One Learning Place . . .

You are coming back to this room . . .
to this time . . .
bringing with you all the wonderful things
you learned there . . .
Knowing you can return to One Learning Place
anytime you wish . . .
simply by closing your eyes
and remembering the trip you took today . . .

When you are ready, slowly open your eyes . . .
Notice that you are feeling relaxed . . . refreshed . . .
and ready to use whatever you learned at One Learning Place.

When everyone has their eyes opened, invite participants to share whatever they wish about their creative visualization experience. Remind the group that creative visualization may take some practice, but it is worth the effort. Suggest to those who were not totally able to get to One Learning Place that they practice the exercise 10 minutes a day for a few weeks. They will be surprised at their progress.

VARIATIONS

Use this exercise whenever participants seem blocked in their ability to learn. By switching from logical thinking to imagery, they may be able to learn more easily. Be sure to use positive suggestion with participants.

Begin the exercise by asking participants to remember a learning experience in which they were uncomfortable, fearful, or embarrassed. Slowly read aloud the following script, pausing after each phrase:

Picture this experience clearly . . .
What are the other people in the situation doing? . . .
What is the trainer doing? . . .
Who is talking to whom? . . .

What are the physical characteristics of the room? . . .
Where are people sitting? . . .
Who is moving? . . .
What is the movement? . . .

What are you thinking? . . .

What are you feeling? . . .

Once you have this unpleasant learning experience clearly in mind, turn it into a pleasant scene . . .

Change other peoples' behavior, facial expression, and words to sound innocuous, maybe even pleasant . . .
Make this a place where you can learn and stay calm . . .

Continue by reading the imagery script in this exercise.

CHECK-IN

In this exercise, after spending a moment in silent personal reflection, participants share their feelings and reactions.

GOALS
To combine internal tuning in with group sharing.
To build cohesiveness and understanding in the group.
To help the leader understand the group's response to the day's activities.

GROUP SIZE
Unlimited.

TIME
15–30 minutes.

MATERIALS
Blank paper; pens or pencils; whistle.

PROCESS
■ Introduce the exercise topic to participants by making the following points:

- Often we speak without thinking and recognize later that our ideas were shallow.

- If we take time to reflect before we speak, our conversations are more likely to be filled with wisdom and insight.

- Today we will have the opportunity to experiment with this process.

Form groups of four to six people. Distribute a piece of paper to each group and provide the following instructions:

- Appoint a recorder in your group to write down whatever the group members share as well as their personal observations.

- We will now take a few minutes for meditation and reflection. With your feet flat on the floor, close your eyes and tune into your feelings.

- What words best describe what you are observing?

- Are you tired? tense? interested? bored? confused?

  Pause for 2 minutes while participants are reflecting.

- Now, open your eyes and tell your group what you observed about yourself. Each group will have only 5 minutes to complete this task, so don't discuss your reactions, merely speak them and help the group recorder get them jotted down. The recorder need not identify who made a comment.

After 5 minutes, collect the recorder's notes. You may read them aloud or wait until the group is involved in another task to look them over. The information you gather can help you design the balance of the workshop activities. Be sure to build in at least an additional 15 minute segment in the training schedule to handle any concerns identified during this exercise.

VARIATIONS

Sit in on one of the groups and respond to group concerns on the spot. Bear in mind that participants may be less candid when you are right there listening. But, if there is a high level of trust and cohesion, this works well.

For large groups, reorganize groups and assign activities based on participants' concerns: tense participants can do a relaxing exercise, hungry participants can take a break and get something to eat, etc.

MY FAVORITE LEARNING ENVIRONMENT

Participants draw individual mandalas signifying important parts of their learning environment.

GOALS

To evaluate the effect of the mandala for providing a different perspective on learning.
To share mandala information with others.

GROUP SIZE

Unlimited.

TIME

30–45 minutes.

MATERIALS

One paper plate for each participant (use a pencil to divide the plate into four equal segments and place a small circle in the center of the plate); colored marking pens; colored pictures from magazines; colored paper; scissors; glue; whistle.

PROCESS

▢ Introduce the exercise by describing mandalas and distribute a paper plate to each participant.

   ▲ A mandala is an expression of the self in relation to the environment. The four equal portions are interrelated parts of the whole.

   ▲ The form of a mandala is a circle. Within the circle are four cardinal points which symbolize anything pertinent to the topic of the mandala.

   ▲ In this exercise, we will create mandalas on the theme of the learning environment.

   ▲ The construction of your mandala can nurture growth and learning by drawing on the right side of the brain to connect learning goals to a creative learning environment.

▢ Place other art materials in a convenient location. Continue by giving the following instructions:

   ▲ Decide what four elements are most important in your learning environment.

   ▲ Place a core value or symbol at the center of the mandala, using images, words, pictures, or drawings.

   ▲ Some suggestions for the four segments are: a personal learning issue, a learning goal you've met or are exceptionally proud of, four words you consider essential to learning, your goal for learning in this session, and aspects of the learning environment that are foremost in your mind. These are only suggestions. You are free to create whatever has meaning to you. Use symbols, pictures, images, or drawings and be sure to use color creatively.

△ I will allow 20 minutes for you to complete your mandala. I'll blow a whistle to signal you when time is up.

▪ While participants are creating their mandala, roam around the groups, encouraging them and answering any questions.

▪ After 20 minutes, call time. Instruct participants to pair up with a partner. Provide the following instructions:

△ Introduce yourself to your partner.

△ Describe the meaning of the core value in the center of your mandala to each other. You will have 2 minutes for this process.

▪ After 2 minutes are up, blow the whistle to call time. Ask the partners to change partners, introduce themselves, and describe to their new partners the meaning of one of the four quadrants in their mandala.

▪ Repeat this process until each of the four quadrants in the mandalas have been discussed.

▪ Reconvene the entire group and ask participants the following questions:

△ What did you place in the center of your plate as the focal point for learning?

△ What information did you place in each of the four quadrants of your mandala?

△ What did you learn about the interaction between the five elements?

△ What effect has creating the learning environment mandala had on your perception of learning?

VARIATION

Form groups of four participants. Each group will create its own mandala, deciding how the four quadrants and the center portion will be designed. At the end of the exercise, each group can display its mandala as a symbol of the group's learning environment.

LEARNING COLLAGE

*Participants use colorful magazine cutouts,
paints, crayons, colored papers, and glue to create
a collage symbolizing their learning experience.*

GOALS
To stimulate reflection on what is being learned.
To work in collaboration with other participants.

GROUP SIZE
Unlimited.

TIME
20–30 minutes.

MATERIALS
Large sheets of tagboard or heavy paper; magazines with colored
pictures; pieces of colorful fabric and string; beads and other decorative items; a pair of scissors for each person; a container of glue
for each group.

PROCESS

Introduce the goals of the exercise and explain that the group is going to create a collage. Begin with the following comments:

- Collage is the art of pasting, sewing, or affixing materials to a surface. It is an art form that awakes us to the potential of everyday things.

- Paper, fabric, string, wire mesh, and miscellaneous objects are commonly used to create collages.

- Collage is an art of reclamation that provides a creative alternative to disposing of objects. It is art's way of recycling.

- Collage is a freeing experience. If you loved cutting and pasting when you were a child, you'll enjoy collage.

- Together, collaboratively, your group will construct a physical representation of your ideas about learning. What was just an idea will expand into a physical reality.

- When you look at your materials, take a minute, close your eyes, and think about how they might represent your learning experience. Lay some objects on the paper and then move them around until they feel right. Find ways to incorporate the ideas of every group member. Avoid letting negative voices stop you. If you change your mind, you can paste another object on top of something, tear it off, or add another object.

- There is no right or wrong way to make a collage. Objects can go on top of each other or colors can be painted on top of words, revealing provocative and cryptic letters. When in doubt, do what feels right. The only rule is don't try to be neat. Now we're ready to begin.

Form groups of four to six participants and distribute one sheet of tagboard and other materials to each group. Let participants know how long they have to work. When time is almost up, encourage groups to finish their collages.

When time is up and the collages are finished, lead a closing discussion using the following questions:

- What are some things you learned about yourself and your group from creating this collage?

- What different perspectives did you get on learning?

- Did you come to some new realizations about learning? What were they?

- What unexpected things did you learn from the collage?

RELAX, GET READY TO LEARN

Participants learn to let go of tensions and worries and immerse themselves in relaxing, peaceful, soothing comfort.

GOALS
To use relaxation as a bridge to an effective learning session.
To let go of tension and worries which may be preventing total concentration on the learning task.

GROUP SIZE
Unlimited.

TIME
15–20 minutes.

MATERIALS
Comfortable chairs or floor space on a carpet or mat.

PROCESS
■ Introduce the exercise goals with the following comments on the importance of structured relaxation:

▲ Did you know that when you came to this session, you brought whatever you've been doing prior to it with you? You may have brought a sense of apprehension or confusion about what we'll be doing . . . about who else will be here and what they will think of you. If you were a few minutes late getting here, you may feel sheepish or worry that you've missed something and are lagging behind. Some of you may have had an angry interchange with a family member, colleague, boss, or driver.

▲ Images and feelings from that encounter may still be reverberating in your brain, body, and soul. You may bring negative feelings about past learning situations or teachers.

▲ A structured relaxation exercise can center, relax, and prepare you to go forward as a group, focused on the here-and-now, extracting the utmost from the training session.

▪ Ask participants to find a comfortable spot, either in their chair or on the floor. Encourage them to relax by loosening tight clothing or kicking off their shoes. While participants are making themselves comfortable, explain that the lights in the room will be dimmed and ask if that will make anyone uncomfortable. If necessary, use a small flashlight or lamp to read the relaxation exercise.

▪ Ask participants to close their eyes or to keep them open if they choose, whatever is most comfortable for them. Read the following script, pausing for a few seconds at each ellipses:

Pay attention to the sensations of your body
against the chair (floor) . . .

Notice the sensation of the chair (floor) against your head . . .
against your shoulders . . . against your arms . . . against your
back . . . against the back of your legs . . .

Breathe in a sense of relaxation . . . a sense of calm and quiet . . . a sense of belonging . . . a sense of clarity in your mind . . .

Let your breathing begin to move lower in your body . . . effortlessly flowing . . . toward your abdomen . . . toward your center . . . easily . . .

Begin to sink into your chair (the floor) . . . paying attention only to the sound of my voice . . . letting any external sounds become part of the relaxation process . . .

You're breathing in peace and contentment . . . perhaps as a color or image . . . you're breathing out whatever you brought here that it's time to let go of . . . perhaps as another color or image . . .

With each exhalation, you are becoming more peaceful, more relaxed, more in tune with learning . . .

Your head is relaxing . . . the next time you inhale, let a wave of relaxation flow over you . . . your scalp is relaxing . . . your hair is relaxing . . . your ears are relaxing . . . your brain is relaxing . . . emptying of all thoughts . . . listening only to the sound of my voice . . . a black velvet curtain is dropping behind your eyes . . . leaving you with a sense of peace and relaxation . . .

If any thoughts come to mind, just let them flow by . . . they have no influence over you . . . if any ideas come back, label them with a time when you will return to them . . . but for now, you are focusing on the sound of my voice and on relaxing . . .

Your forehead is relaxing . . . smoothing out . . . your eyebrows are relaxing . . . your eyelashes are relaxing . . . your eyes are relaxing and the space behind that and the space behind that . . .

Creating a Climate for Power Learning

*Your cheeks are relaxing . . . your jaw is relaxing . . . unlock
your jaw and let your mouth open an inch or so . . . breathing
easily . . . effortlessly . . . your teeth are relaxing . . . your
tongue is relaxing . . . your throat is relaxing . . . soothed by a
cool refreshing wave of relaxation each time you inhale . . .*

*Your neck is relaxing . . . all the muscles and bones and
ligaments are floating along . . . relaxing . . .*

*With your next breath, let a wave of relaxation flow over
you . . . over your shoulders . . . all the muscles in your
shoulders are relaxing . . . spreading out . . . taking up all the
space there is for them to relax into . . . let any worries or
thoughts or whatever you've been carrying around on your
shoulders just roll right across your shoulders, down your
arms and out your fingertips . . .*

*Your back is relaxing . . . each vertebra is relaxing . . .
one . . . by one . . . by one . . . and all the muscles and bones
and nerves and ligaments in your back are relaxing . . .
spreading out and taking up all that quiet, peaceful space
there is available . . .*

*Your buttocks are relaxing into the chair (the floor) . . .
each layer of muscles in your buttocks is relaxing . . . layer,
by layer, by layer . . . let that sense of relaxation just flow
down your back . . . down your legs and out your toes . . .
knowing that the next time you inhale, you will be breathing
in even more relaxation . . .*

*Now turn your attention to the front of your body . . .
your chest is relaxing . . . your heart is relaxing . . . your
lungs are relaxing . . . spreading out, looking healthy, taking up
all the space that is available in your chest for them to use . . .*

All your internal organs, your stomach, your liver . . . your pancreas . . . your intestines . . . your kidneys . . . all your internals organs are relaxing . . . feeling healthy . . . working well . . . keeping you well . . . picture all your insides a healthy pink color, perfect in function, comfortable . . .

Now move slowly down your body . . . pausing a moment in your
groin area . . . picture it relaxing . . . feeling healthy . . .

Now move slowly down your body . . . feeling your legs beginning to relax . . . all the muscles, bones, and ligaments are relaxing . . . layer, by layer, by layer . . . front, back, side . . . your knees are relaxing, sinking or floating, whichever has meaning for you . . . your lower legs are relaxing . . . your ankles are relaxing . . . your feet are relaxing . . . top . . . bottom . . . sides . . . each toe . . .

On your next breath, let a wave of relaxation flow from your head all the way down the outside and inside of your body . . .

(pause 10 seconds)

Scan your body now and find any areas that need to be more relaxed . . . on your next breath, send a wave of relaxation to those places . . . relaxing . . . calming . . . peace . . .

(pause at least 15 seconds)

Now, in the distance, you begin to see a comforting white light . . . it comes closer . . . flowing over you . . . filling you up with the light of knowledge and information . . . a healing light . . . a light which will guide and comfort you every step of your learning experience today . . . a light which will help you remember the important things you want to remember from today's learning experience . . .

(add any other suggestions appropriate to learning or remembering for today's session)

I want you to remember the pleasant feelings, the peace, the clarity in your mind and carry that with you through your day today, knowing you can return to these sensations anytime you want merely by picturing yourself in this room, in this spot, listening to my voice . . .

Now open your eyes slowly and get ready to learn . . .

VARIATION

Record the relaxation script, practicing until it sounds just right to you. Then when participants are relaxing, you can be relaxing too, preparing yourself for a calm, peaceful, but stimulating session.

ADMIT ONE TO LEARNING

In this exercise, participants are given tickets stubs to fill out with the questions they would like answered during the session.

GOALS
To engage participants in the learning process.
To gain information about participant needs in a safe, nonthreatening way.

GROUP SIZE
Unlimited.

TIME
5–7 minutes.

MATERIALS
Ticket to Learning—photocopy the tickets printed at the end of this exercise; a hat, box, or bucket for collecting tickets.

PROCESS
■ Distribute a ticket to each participant upon entry into the

training session. When everyone is seated, make the following comments:

- To help me tailor this workshop to your needs, I'd like to know what you hope to learn today.

- I would like each of you to think of two questions that you would like to have answered in this session. Write those questions on your **Ticket to Learning.**

- Although no question is out of bounds if it relates to the learning topic, be aware that it may be presented to the class anonymously for discussion. You will have 3 minutes to write your two questions.

After 3 minutes, collect the tickets by passing around a container to the group.

When participants are working on another exercise, scan the responses and see if certain questions recur. If so, be sure to cover that information during your session or at least give participants some direction for finding the answers themselves after the session.

If you are conducting an ongoing training group, you can use the questions as discussion starters or as a guide for information to be presented in upcoming sessions.

TICKET TO LEARNING

1. _____

_____

2. _____

_____

TICKET TO LEARNING

1. _____

_____

2. _____

_____

TICKET TO LEARNING

1. _____

_____

2. _____

_____

TICKET TO LEARNING

1. _____

_____

2. _____

_____

CREATING A LEARNING STORY

Participants learn the importance of cooperation
with others by creating a learning story.
Each person adds a sentence to develop the story.

GOALS

To share ideas about essentials for effective learning.
To cooperate with other participants in a fun activity.

GROUP SIZE

Unlimited. If there are more than 20 participants, form small groups
of 5–7 people.

TIME

15–30 minutes.

MATERIALS

A copy of either **Ken's Learning Story** or **Karen's Learning Story**
for each group; pens or pencils.

PROCESS

Introduce the topic of learning experiences with the following comments:

- Participants arrive at a workshop with a variety of expectations.

- Some are happy to be there; others would prefer to be elsewhere.

- Some anticipate an exciting workshop, during which they will learn many new things; others expect to be bored or fear they will be embarrassed.

- To help understand what makes a person eager to learn, you will work together to develop the story of two workshop participants with very different expectations.

Form two or more groups, each with three to seven participants. Distribute copies of **Karen's Learning Story** to half the groups and **Ken's Learning Story** to the other half, then provide the following instructions:

- I will introduce Ken and Karen's stories, then the youngest person in your group will fill in the first blank line on the worksheet, fold the page back on the first dotted line, and pass it to the right. Each person will fill in one blank, fold the page again, and pass it to the right. You will have 10 minutes to complete the story.

- Ken and Karen were both scheduled to attend today's workshop. Ken was reluctant to be here, but Karen was eager to participate. Last night they both dreamed about the experience they anticipated. As you complete your worksheets, you will tell their stories.

After 10 minutes, reconvene the group. Ask volunteers to read their group's story, then conclude the exercise by asking several of the following questions:

- What past experiences may have given Ken and Karen such differing expectations for this workshop?

- To what extent do you think their expectations affected their actual learning experience?

- How important to you are the physical arrangements for a workshop?

- What balance of lecture and experiential activities helps you learn most effectively?

- What is the one most important thing a facilitator should do when planning a learning experience?

KAREN'S LEARNING STORY

In her dream, Karen approached today's workshop eagerly because she anticipated _____

_____

She found an ideal learning space, furnished _____

_____

The facilitator made Karen feel comfortable by _____

_____

The exciting learning processes included _____

_____

Other students added to the fun by _____

_____

During the day Karen learned _____

_____

Karen left the workshop feeling _____

_____

©1997 Carolyn Chambers Clark Whole Person Associates • 210 West Michigan • Duluth, MN 55802 • (800) 247-6789

Creating a Climate for Power Learning

©1997 Carolyn Chambers Clark • Whole Person Associates • 210 West Michigan • Duluth, MN 55802 • (800) 247-6789

KEN'S LEARNING STORY

In his dream, Ken approached today's workshop reluctantly

because he anticipated _____

_____

He found a disagreeable learning space, furnished _____

_____

The facilitator made Ken feel uncomfortable by _____

_____

The boring learning processes included _____

_____

Other students added to the unpleasant atmosphere by _____

_____

During the day Ken learned _____

_____

Ken left the workshop feeling _____

_____

LEARNING CHEER

This lively exercise helps participants identify and enthusiastically support favorite ways to enhance learning.

GOALS

To identify ways to enhance a learning environment.
To share ideas with other participants.

GROUP SIZE

Unlimited.

TIME

15–30 minutes.

MATERIALS

Empty toilet paper rolls for each participant; easel paper and markers; masking tape.

PROCESS

■ Form groups of four to six participants and introduce the session by making the following comments:

△ We all have favorite ways of learning. You may listen to music; others require complete silence. You may prefer to sit at a desk; teens often flop on a bed. You may learn best by reading, while another member of your group needs hands-on experience.

△ In this exercise, you will list the ways you prefer to learn.

△ Select a recorder to write your group's ideas on easel paper. You will have 15 minutes for this brainstorming process.

▫ While the groups are brainstorming, roam around the room, cheering them on or hurrying them along. Think of creative ways to use your toilet paper roll megaphone that will add to the fun of this exercise.

▫ After 15 minutes, distribute toilet paper roll megaphones. Ask each group to develop a cheer for their most creative idea.

▫ After 5 minutes, reconvene the entire group and collect the notes from each group's recorder. Tape the notes to the wall where they can be read by everyone. Encourage participants to try some new ideas for learning during the rest of the training session.

▫ Ask each group to use their megaphones and present their cheer.

> *If you have ongoing sessions with this group, you may type up the notes and give copies to each participant.*

VARIATION

▫ Read aloud the lists of learning techniques. Ask participants to raise their hands if they use a specific technique. This can help you design training experiences that fit participant needs.

THE FEEDBACK LOOP

Participants practice using a constant feedback system to arrive at the solution to a problem.

GOALS
To practice the feedback process of problem-solving.
To participate in a fun exercise while learning a new skill.

GROUP SIZE
Unlimited.

TIME
20–45 minutes.

MATERIALS
Easel paper and markers for each group; masking tape; colored markers.

PROCESS
Introduce the exercise by introducing the feedback system of problem-solving with the following comments:

- Problem-solving is a creative, constructive process. Housewives, hula dancers, internet users, basketball players, doctors, lawyers, students, and even facilitators use this process, so why shouldn't you?

- Consider a basketball team. The players listen to the coach, practice strategies, see how they work, modify them, use them in a game, analyze them, and modify them again. The feedback loop is continual. Teams that don't learn from feedback lose.

- The first step in problem solving is to accept the situation. In the case of this training session, we must accept the problem of learning about (**topic of training session**). Think of it as a challenge, better yet, as a case of surrender. You must surrender to the problem, allowing the problem to take over and become your process. If you don't believe you have a problem, you'll never solve it.

Ask participants to form groups of six to eight members to begin the first step in the problem solving process, then give the following instructions.

- The person whose last name begins with "A" take notes on the easel paper. Record all the ideas that are offered. The rest of the group will brainstorm ten to twenty ways to accept the problem. Be sure not to censor any ideas. They're all valuable. You will have 5 minutes for this process.

Call time after 5 minutes, then continue with the following instructions:

- The second step in the problem-solving process is analysis—getting to know everything possible about the problem. Without accurate information, you cannot arrive at a good solution.

▲ First identify at least five ways—the more creative the better to analyze the problem, then use one or more of those techniques and list everything you can about this problem.

If participants have difficulty with this process, be prepared to help them by suggesting a few examples, such as looking at the problem from a completely different perspective, working from the parts toward the whole or the whole toward the parts, or drawing an analogy (comparing the problem to something else).

Call time in 5 minutes, then tell participants the next step in the problem-solving process is to define the major issues. Use what you learned in the previous step—that's the feedback—and define the major issues for this problem. Don't censor any ideas, write them all down, but focus on defining what's *really* important.

After 5 minutes, call time and give the next instruction:

▲ The next step in the problem-solving process is to ideate—searching out alternatives or different ways to solve the problem. Take 5 minutes to list at least ten alternate ways to reach a solution to this problem. Again, be creative. Look at your responses to the previous steps. Don't censor or judge any ideas, just write them down. The more, the better.

Call time in 5 minutes and continue with the next instruction:

▲ The next step in the problem-solving process it to select—to determine the best option from the alternatives you brainstormed. Not all ideas are practical. Some are fun and creative, but they're too expensive, too difficult, or they just won't work. From your list of possible solutions, select the best one and decide why you think it will work.

After 5 minutes, call time and tell the group:

▲ You've accepted the situation, analyzed it, defined it, searched out alternatives, and selected the best one. Now it is time for action. Take 5 minutes to write a detailed plan for how to implement your solution to the problem I posed.

▪ After 5 minutes, present the final step to the group:

▲ The final step in the problem-solving process is to evaluate. In this important step, you will review all the previous steps and evaluate the results of your actions. Identify at least three ways to evaluate the results of your actions. If possible, try out your solution to the problem and see how it works. If that's not possible, imagine seeing the solution in action, then evaluate what's right and wrong with the solution.

▪ After 5 minutes, reconvene the entire group and lead a closing discussion:

▲ You have gone through all the problem-solving steps using feedback from each step to help with the next one. Is it that easy in real life? No. Many times you have to define the problem before you can analyze it or accept it. Likewise, sometimes you have to go back and select another goal when you find out the one you chose won't work.

▲ What did you learn about the value of the feedback loop from doing this exercise?

▲ How can you use the feedback loop in learning?

▲ How can you use the feedback loop in your work?

▲ What suggestions do you have for making a feedback system part of your life?

THE EMPEROR'S NEW LEARNING CLOTHES

In this dress-up exercise, participants choose vests, hats, jewelry, and other accessories they believe will enhance their learning experience.

GOALS
To recall and enjoy the pleasure of wearing a costume.
To identify how clothing can affect our feelings about ourselves and our ability to learn.

GROUP SIZE
Unlimited except by the number of costume accessories. If a large group is expected, ask each participant to bring a hat, vest, jewelry, or any type of clothing to use as a prop in this exercise.

TIME
15–40 minutes.

MATERIALS
Vests, caps, jewelry, scarves, etc.—enough so that each person gets at least one accessory to wear.

PROCESS

▪ If participants have brought items of clothing and accessories, ask them to place the items on a table and then to be seated.

▪ When everyone is seated, encourage participants to think back to a time in their childhood when they played dress-up. Ask the group the following questions:

 ▲ What kinds of costumes did you wear?

 ▲ How did you act differently when you were in costume?

 ▲ Why do you think you acted differently?

 ▲ Were the changes in your behavior positive?

 ▲ What did you enjoy about dressing up that might encourage you to put a little more fun in your life now?

▪ After the group has finished discussing these questions, invite participants to go to the display table and find at least one accessory to wear for the rest of the session that they believe will help them learn.

▪ Once everyone is wearing at least one accessory, ask participants to allow their costume to affect their interactions throughout the day.

▪ Suggest that participants who wish they had additional accessories pretend they are wearing the accessory, just like the emperor who was naked but believed he was wearing a new suit of clothes.

 ▲ How do you feel different now that you are wearing the accessory?

- How are you acting different now that you are wearing the accessory?

- If there were more accessories, what else would you choose to wear and why?

VARIATIONS

- Have materials available, including paper, fabric, etc., so participants can make additional props.

- If there is time at the workshop's conclusion, ask participants to note any changes they observed in their learning style that could be attributed to their costumes.

LEARNING CREATIVELY

Get the participants' creative juices flowing by offering a wide variety of imaginative processes.

THE ZEN OF LEARNING

*Participants choose personal process
mottos to help in their learning.*

GOALS
To promote sharing of creative learning ideas.
To focus attention on the process of learning.

GROUP SIZE
Unlimited.

TIME
15–45 minutes.

MATERIALS
Paper; crayons or colored marking pens.

PROCESS
▪ Introduce the exercise topic and invite participants to put on
their creativity hats.

■ Distribute paper and crayons or colored marking pens to participants. Provide the following instructions:

▲ There is an old Zen motto that says, "If you want to get someplace, you've got to give up wanting to get there." That translates into if you want to achieve something, you've got to get into the process of achieving it. You've got to find out what makes it tick, what's inside it, how the parts interrelate. You've got to give up on focusing on the final goal and instead become enthralled with the process of moving toward that goal.

■ Read the script that follows slowly, pausing after each phrase.

At this time I would like you to take a few minutes to relax and imagine yourself deeply involved in the process of learning.

Forget about grades, credits, and diplomas.

Forget about what you should learn and imagine yourself immersed in what you'd love to learn.

When you are ready, pick up your crayons and draw a picture that in some way expresses the Zen of learning. Add a motto to your drawing.

■ As soon as everyone has finished their drawings, invite participants to share their picture and motto with others in the group Allow 2 minutes each for this process.

WHO I AM?

In this exercise, participants meditate on the meaning of their names.

GOALS
To explore how names affect behavior.
To use a self-affirming meditation to enhance feelings of well-being and prepare for learning.

GROUP SIZE
Unlimited.

TIME
15–35 minutes.

MATERIALS
Relaxing music; cassette player; floor mats or a carpeted room (optional) for participants who want to lie down and meditate.

PROCESS
This exercise is especially useful when the group has been very active (as a contrast) or when members of the group are under

stress. It can also be used advantageously any time during the learning experience when you think the group could benefit from inner reflection.

▦ Introduce the exercise and provide the following instructions:

⬧ Find a comfortable position. You may remain in your chair or you may lie down on the floor (or floor mats).

⬧ As soon as everyone is comfortable, I will dim the lights and turn on some relaxing music. Feel free to loosen tight clothing, kick off your shoes, and close your eyes.

▦ Read the following script slowly, pausing at each ellipses:

Let your breathing move effortlessly to your center, your abdominal area. You might want to picture your breath coming in as a soothing color . . . and going out as another color, taking with it anything it's time to let go of, whatever you don't need anymore . . .

Notice how easy and effortlessly you're breathing . . . the sensation of your back against the chair (floor) . . . drifting along . . . letting any thoughts flow by . . . focusing only on my voice and what I'm saying . . .

If any thoughts persist, note them with a time you will come back to them . . . but for now, you are relaxing, listening to me . . .

(pause for 10 seconds)

Names are important, they are our identity . . . our guide for who we are and how we act . . . take a minute or two now to picture your name and what it means to you . . . say your name aloud or in your mind . . .

Let images come before you . . . positive images of what your name is about . . . ask yourself, who am I? . . . keep asking gently until you get an answer . . . effortlessly, the answer appears before you . . . as if a movie on screen . . .

Picture yourself on the movie screen in positive learning situations . . . using what you know and what you can do . . . what you believe . . .

Observe how your name . . . your identity reflects what you believe . . .

Focus on the images . . . smell the smells . . . hear the sounds . . . feel the sensations . . . see whatever there is to see . . . every detail . . .

Remembering the positive image of your name and who you are . . . let the positive feelings about your name and identity flow through you . . . absorb the wonderful feeling of knowing your name and being the person you are . . .

Now, gradually, comfortably, return to this room . . . to this place . . . bringing with you everything you learned . . . the good feelings and images associated with you and your name . . . gradually . . . easily . . . open your eyes and keep with you those positive feelings about your name and your identity . . .

Know that you can recapture a sense of positive learning and identity merely by picturing yourself in this room . . . imagining yourself in positive learning experiences . . .

Lead a closing discussion by asking participants to share what they learned during the meditation.

VARIATIONS

- Ask participants to select a partner and share with each other what they learned.

- Ask participants to spend 2 minutes writing about what they learned during the meditation and how they might use what they learned in today's session and in the future.

THE LEARNING PUZZLE

*Participants collaborate to create a puzzle, each of
them supplying a piece of information they hope to learn.*

GOALS

To identify learning tasks in the current session.
To collaborate with the larger group on a learning task.

GROUP SIZE

Unlimited, but a small group works best.

TIME

15–20 minutes.

MATERIALS

Dark-colored marking pens, one for each group member; one puzzle
for each group. (Prior to the session, draw on a piece of white
cardboard or very heavy paper the outline of an object relevant to
the upcoming session. You might, for example, draw the outline of
a computer for a word processing class or the outline of a mother
holding an infant for a parenting class.) On the outline, draw enough
puzzle pieces for each participant in the group or small groups to

have one. Cut out the pieces and place each set in an envelope. Label each envelope: The Learning Puzzle.

PROCESS

Introduce the exercise topic with the following comments:

- Collaboration is a lot like putting together a puzzle.

- Each piece (or person) is important to the complete picture. The puzzle isn't complete if a single piece is missing; the collaboration isn't effective unless everyone participates.

- Today, we are going to collaborate to define our learning goals and to put together a puzzle.

Form small groups of four to six participants. Distribute one of the envelopes containing a puzzle to each group along with enough markers for each person in the group. Provide the following directions:

- Whoever is holding the envelope for your group can now open your group's envelope and spread out the pieces. Choose a puzzle piece and on it write with a marker your most important learning goal for today.

- Think hard about your most important learning goal and be as specific as possible.

- When you're finished, place your piece on the table. All of the pieces combined will form a picture, so interlock your piece with everyone else's piece to form an outline that relates to today's session.

Circulate around the room to monitor the process and help groups maintain a similar pace. When everyone is finished, ask group members to decide how they can help each other meet the goals they selected.

VARIATIONS

If you have more than one group, have members of each group examine the other groups' puzzles. Lead a discussion about what they learned from seeing the other puzzles.

Glue the puzzle pieces down on a sheet of paper or cardboard and hang them around the room or in front of each group as inspiration for the day's activities.

Ask group members to sign a contract stating that they will help each other meet the learning goals.

THINGS I KNOW FOR SURE

This fast-paced exercise gives participants a chance to consider information they never thought about before and provides an opportunity for a succession of contacts with other group members and their ideas.

GOALS

To hear about positive learning experiences.
To promote self-disclosure and interaction among participants.

GROUP SIZE

Unlimited.

TIME

10–20 minutes.

MATERIALS

One whistle; chips or strips of paper in several colors, ten for each participant; ten prizes that would be useful during the learning session, such as writing pens, marking pens, Post-it notes, etc.

PROCESS

▪ Introduce the goals of the exercise to the group. Give each participant ten chips or strips of paper in varying colors. Provide the following instructions:

    ▴ Find a partner and decide who will listen first and who will talk. Talkers, when I blow the whistle, tell your partner about a situation in which you learned something positive, impressive, or useful. Listener, if that information was new to you, give the talker a chip (or strip of paper). You will have 2 minutes for this process.

    ▴ After 2 minutes, I will blow the whistle a second time. Listeners, you are now the talkers. Share a positive learning experience with your partner, who will give you a chip (or strip of paper) if the information is new. You will have 2 minutes for sharing.

    ▴ After 2 minutes, I will blow the whistle a third time. At this time, both partners will find new partners to begin the process all over again.

▪ After giving the above directions, ask participants to begin the process and inform them that you will blow the whistle after 2 minutes. Circulate around the group to make sure they are following the directions.

▪ After the first pair has shared their ideas, blow the whistle and make sure they find new partners. Don't be shy about blowing the whistle. It adds to the fun and helps participants relax.

▪ At the end, ask participants to count their chips or slips of paper. Award prizes, making sure that everyone gets a prize for the most chips, least chips, most yellow chips, most red chips, etc.

VARIATION

■ Form groups of four to eight participants. Ask each person to take a turn telling about a positive learning experience.

Creating a Climate for Power Learning

ESCAPE TO LEARNING

*In brief role plays, participants explore the difficult
and challenging situations in which many people live.*

GOALS

To put a difficult learning task in perspective.
To encourage imagination and creativity.

GROUP SIZE

Unlimited.

TIME

30–45 minutes.

MATERIALS

A variety of hats and other props that fit the following roles: religious leader; president of the United States; mother of a blind and deaf child; brain surgeon; resident of a nursing home; homeless person; Zen monk; head of the Environmental Protection Agency; political candidate speaking to a booing and hissing group; a dog trying to communicate with his master. Write these and other demanding roles on slips of paper. If you plan to form small groups with eight participants, you will need to select eight roles. Duplicate the slips for each group.

PROCESS

- Introduce the exercise topic with a brief chalktalk on the concerns participants might have about learning the material that will be presented in the workshop.

  - Responsible people take very seriously the obligation to learn everything possible from a workshop or class.

  - Sometimes their concerns can actually get in the way of effective learning.

  - We're going to take a few minutes to put our responsibilities in perspective.

  - The responsibilities that go with learning the content of this session are actually easy when compared to those that many people carry every day.

  - The president of the United States, a Supreme Court justice, an inner city police officer, the mother of a blind and deaf child, or the head of the Environmental Protection Agency all carry responsibilities way beyond what you need to do to learn the information that will be presented in this training session.

  - Imagining all the headaches of a really tough situation can help you appreciate how easy it's going to be for you to learn what you need to in today's session.

- Instruct the large group to form smaller groups of no more than ten people. Distribute the demanding role titles to each group, then provide the following instructions:

- On the slips of paper that I distributed, you will find some very demanding roles. Select one of the props, then use it to help you act out your role.

- You will each have 2 minutes to demonstrate how difficult and stressful this role is.

- After everyone in your group has had a turn, discuss among yourselves the feelings you had during your role play while you wait for the other groups to finish.

When all the groups are done with the role plays, reconvene the entire group and lead a closing discussion by asking participants to compare the task of mastering the workshop's content with the responsibilities and obligations they just saw demonstrated.

HOW IS AN ORANGE LIKE A BAROMETER?

*In this exercise, participants learn how two objects
that appear unrelated can be similar to one another.*

GOALS
To expand creative thinking by examining new relationships.
To promote one-to-one interaction.

GROUP SIZE
Unlimited.

TIME
15–25 minutes.

MATERIALS
Two objects for each pair of participants—materials can vary from
can openers to elastic bands; a carrying container for your items;
blank paper; pencils or pens; a whistle.

PROCESS

Introduce the exercise with the following chalktalk:

- One way to promote creative thinking is to ask, "How is this thing like that thing?" By asking the question and being open to the answer, similarities never considered before are uncovered. New viewpoints arise.

- In a problem-solving situation, we could explore how to get a toddler to fall asleep, for instance, then ask how the process we used could help us design a better way to run staff meetings.

- In this training session, our problem is to learn (**state a goal or purpose of the training session**). Let's see how this process could help us.

- First, let's explore how two unrelated items might be similar.

- For example, how is an apple like a rowboat?

If you like, let the group shout out answers for this first pair of items so they get the idea of how to proceed.

If participants can't generate any answers to the question, provide the following explanation:

- An apple and a rowboat both use energy when being transported. The apple uses a truck's or a person's energy moving from a farm or an orchard to the table. The rowboat uses a person's energy to move through the water. Also, they both transport energy. The apple is a source of nutrition to the body.

Ask participants to select a partner and find an area where they can work. Distribute two items from your container to each pair along with a sheet of blank paper. Provide the following instructions:

- Place your two items in clear view. Take 3 minutes to brainstorm five ways in which the items are alike.

- Write your responses on your sheet of paper to later report to the group. I will blow the whistle after 3 minutes.

- Reconvene the entire group and ask participants to comment on the process, the results, and the fun.

- Lead the group through a brainstorming process similar to the one just completed, comparing the goal of the workshop to a dissimilar problem.

- Conclude the exercise by asking the group for insights about this process.

VARIATIONS

- Have each pair exchange items with another pair. During the larger group sharing, have the two pairs present their findings as a small group and tell what they learned from listening to the other partner's findings.

- After reconvening the group, give the items that were used in the brainstorming as prizes, including: best ideas, worst ideas, funniest ideas, silliest ideas, most likely to succeed ideas, and so on, until all items have been given out.

I'M A CHICKEN PLUCKIN', ORANGE PEELIN', SO-AND-SO

Participants use role playing as a creative encounter to gain deeper insight and new perspectives.

GOALS

To use role playing as a creative encounter.
To gain deeper insight and new perspectives.

GROUP SIZE

Unlimited. An even number is suggested, but if there is an uneven number, have the additional person work with one of the pairs.

TIME

15–30 minutes.

MATERIALS

Slips of paper with role-playing situations written out on them ahead of time such as: chicken being plucked, computer being word processed, report being written, orange being peeled, car being driven, cake being baked, movie being made, student being tutored, shoe being worn, shirt being sewn, or house being painted; container for cards or slips of paper; whistle; blank paper; pens or pencils.

PROCESS

▓ Introduce the exercise by outlining the following concepts:

▲ One way to encourage your own creativity is to role-play.

▲ It's not a great stretch to pretend that you are plucking a chicken, but in this exercise you may be asked to become the chicken that is being plucked.

So you know the group understands the task, ask a volunteer to pretend that he or she is a chicken being plucked. This will loosen up the group and let them see that it's all right to be silly and have fun while learning.

▓ When the laughter subsides, continue by providing the following instructions:

▲ Find a partner, someone you don't know well. As I pass around this container, draw a slip of paper. Each paper contains a role-playing situation for you to act out. Don't let your partner see your paper.

▲ Select which partner will begin the role play. The other partner is to observe the role play and try to guess what situation is being portrayed.

▲ After 5 minutes, I will blow the whistle to call time and you will switch roles with your partner.

▓ After 10 minutes, reconvene the entire group. If time is available, allow a few eager actors to present their role plays to this larger audience. Conclude with a discussion of some of the following questions:

- What did it feel like to be an object acted upon rather than a person performing an action?

- Did you as an actor or an observer feel empathy for the object being portrayed in an uncomfortable situation?

- How could this exercise help you manage a situation in which you must learn how to use a piece of equipment?

- How could the insights you gained from this exercise help you in your daily life?

VARIATIONS

- For a longer exercise and more practice in role-playing creative relationships, have the partners draw two slips of paper each.

- Instead of choosing partners, have participants act out their role play in front of the entire group. This works well when the group is already warmed up.

WHAT IS A FIREPLACE TABLE?

*Participants discover that forcing
relationships encourages creative thinking.*

GOALS
To find new ways of understanding relationships.
To have fun while being creative.

GROUP SIZE
Unlimited.

TIME
15–30 minutes.

MATERIALS
Slips of paper with two items listed on them in the form of a question: "What would result if you combined ___ with ___?"; paper; pens or pencils; whistle; a container; prizes (optional).

PROCESS
Introduce the exercise goals with the following comments:

- Forced relationship is a way to provoke creative thought. In this technique, you ask what would result if you combined two unrelated items together. The conclusions provide deeper insight into the way both things work.

- For example, what would happen if we joined a fireplace and a table? If the table sat inside the fireplace, we could eat in cozy comfort. If the fireplace sat on the table we could flip burgers with ease. If the table surrounded the fireplace, you could start a trendy restaurant. Forcing relationships creates endless possibilities if you use your imagination.

- When we force a relationship between two unrelated items, we ask the question, "What would result if we combined or joined this thing to that thing?" The conclusions that result provide deeper insight into the roles each item plays in the joining.

Give the group an example by holding up two different items and asking the following question:

- What would result if I combined (**hold up one item**) with (**hold up the second item**)?

Encourage the group until at least a dozen different ideas have been generated. Then provide participants with the following instructions:

- Select a partner and find a place to work without interference from the other pairs.

- As I pass around a container of slips of paper with questions on them, each pair will select one slip of paper.

- Brainstorm with your partner creative ideas in response to the question on your paper. You will have 10 minutes for this time of creativity.

- As participants are writing their responses, circulate among the pairs, making sure they understand the assignment.

- After 10 minutes, call time and collect the responses in a container. Read aloud some of the responses that were generated by the pairs and ask for additional ideas. Lead a closing discussion about the benefits of this process.

VARIATIONS

- Have two participants work independently on the same two items. When time is up, ask those participants to compare their answers, either in pairs or in front of the group.

- Ask the group to vote and award prizes for: the best forced relationship ideas, the silliest, the most useful, the most likely to succeed, the most potentially lucrative, etc. Use your creativity to gather enough inexpensive prizes and reasons to receive a prize so that everyone in the group is awarded one.

THE MIND RULES

This experiment vividly demonstrates to participants how thoughts can interfere with the learning process.

GOALS

To demonstrate how attitudes, thoughts, and feelings can lead to a positive or negative learning experience.
To brainstorm ways to stay positive about learning goals.

GROUP SIZE

Unlimited.

TIME

10–20 minutes.

MATERIALS

Easel pad; markers.

PROCESS

Introduce the exercise goals to participants and ask for a volunteer from the group for a quick demonstration. Provide the volunteer with the following instructions:

- Hold your right arm out to your side at shoulder level.

- Now I want you to think "I am powerful and brilliant" while I gently push down for a second or two on your wrist.

- While you are pushing down on the volunteer's wrist, comment to the group on the volunteer's strength. After the group takes note of the strength the volunteer is showing at this time, give the following instruction to the volunteer:

  - Now hold your arm up at shoulder level and resist me when I push down on your wrist. While you are resisting me, repeat these words aloud several times, "I am weak and not very smart."

- While the volunteer is repeating the statements, gently push down for a second or two on their wrist. Discuss with the volunteer the change in strength and how the mind rules the body and its strength.

  Although this process usually works, if the volunteer decides to resist the suggestion, it may fail. Be prepared to laugh, then praise the volunteer's strength of will.

- Ask for a second volunteer and repeat the process. Discuss any differences that you or group members notice.

- After the second demonstration, ask the volunteers to be seated and lead a group discussion using the following questions:

  - How can negativity, our own or other people's, weaken us?

  - How can thinking and speaking positively have a positive effect on our bodies?

Brainstorm ideas with participants about ways everyone can keep positive about today's session. Write the ideas generated on the easel pad. Encourage group members to think of other ways to remind ourselves to have a positive attitude every day.

EARTH ANGEL

Participants get a special assist from
their personal guardian angels.

GOALS
To enhance imagination.
To promote small group interaction and bonding.

GROUP SIZE
Unlimited.

TIME
10–40 minutes.

MATERIALS
Assorted colored construction paper; pens; one pair of scissors for each participant; cotton, feathers, sparkle, sequins, etc.

> *Some people may have religious objections to this exercise. Be*
> *prepared with an alternate activity.*

PROCESS
Introduce the exercise goals and make the following comment:

▲ I would like each of you to believe that you have a guardian angel who spends all day, every day, watching over and encouraging you. The potential of that angel is just waiting to be unleashed. All you have to do is call upon it.

▓ Ask participants to find a relaxing position and close their eyes for a brief visualization sequence. Read aloud the following script, pausing briefly after each phrase:

Close your eyes, and imagine your guardian angel, . . .
someone to help you learn what you need to learn.

Visualize yourself flying in the sky with your personal angel.
Notice how light and feathery you feel.
Notice how it makes you want to smile.

Angels come in all sizes, shapes, and types.
Yours is perfect for you.

Perhaps yours is a cheerleading angel
who will cheer you on as you learn.

Maybe your angel is a comedian, always ready to play
practical jokes on you and keep you laughing.

Angel psychologists can help you figure out
what's blocking you from learning.

What does your angel look like . . . sound like . . . feel like.
Imagine your angel's name . . . and take a few moments to
converse with your angel.

Hold these images of your angel in your mind.
Now open your eyes.
You are ready to learn—with the help of your guardian angel.

▓ When everyone has their eyes open, distribute the construction paper, scissors, and decorating materials. Ask each person to construct a personal angel.

When they are finished constructing their angels, ask the group to list ways they can work with their personal angel during the day's learning session.

VARIATIONS

Whenever the group seems resistant to learning, ask them to have their guardian angel write to your guardian angel and suggest ways you can help them learn the necessary information.

Make a deck of angel cards. List one positive quality per card: joy, humor, peace, light, surrender, trust, wisdom, determination, etc. Include two blank cards which participants can use to request a specific quality you didn't think of. Have each person draw a card, then tell the other group members how that quality could help them in today's learning tasks. For groups larger than fifteen members, form smaller groups.

PERSONAL LEARNING JOURNAL

Using a journal as a focus for learning,
participants chart their learning experience.

GOALS
To tap inner resources to find connections, open learning blocks, and understand complex relationships.
To discuss the use of a journal for learning.

GROUP SIZE
Unlimited.

TIME
10–30 minutes.

MATERIALS
Journals or notebooks for each participant; pens or pencils.

PROCESS
▪ Introduce the exercise and present the following chalktalk on the benefits of journaling:

If participants are experienced at journaling, you might elicit the following points through discussion.

- Journal writing is a dialogue with yourself. Flow writing (stream of consciousness) is the basic form of writing used in journaling. Writing flows between the responding mind and the writer and back again. Thoughts rise up and become verbal expressions that tumble onto the page.

- Journal writing allows people to reclaim parts of themselves that have been denied, underrated, or discarded. These parts, once recovered, can assist in the learning process and can provide additional kinds of learning.

- Journal writing allows for privacy, yet provides opportunities for group support. You can volunteer to read aloud from your journal, but you have the responsibility of writing and reading to yourself, not of interacting with or directly responding to others' readings.

- Creative people tend to experience their lives in terms of active and multiple miniprocesses rather than as static events. Entries in a daily log can provide a sense of continuity and stability since outer events often seem chaotic and ever changing.

- Journal writing is especially useful when people are at a crossroad point or transition, when a decision needs to be made, or something new is to be learned.

- Entries at the end of a set of learning experiences can be used to integrate new learnings and insights.

- Journal writing can help clarify and underline a particularly difficult, important, or gratifying relationship with a peer, trainer, or boss.

- Journal writing can be used throughout a job experience to evaluate and integrate work experiences.

- Journal writing can be used in anticipation of a particularly difficult experience to prepare, understand, and remove potential blocks.

When you are finished presenting the above chalktalk, distribute writing materials and provide the following instructions to participants:

- Prior to writing, remain silent and center yourself on the activity, keeping your breathing slow and deep, perhaps closing your eyes for a moment to focus on yourself.

- Begin to write about yourself and your experiences with learning.

- Avoid a conscious effort to think about learning, instead invoke a relaxed attitude, remaining open and receptive.

- Date your entry and begin to write in a nonjudgmental, noncensoring fashion. You will have 10 minutes.

After 10 minutes, ask participants to pause and silently read what they recorded. Ask them to add any additional material that will clarify or deepen their writing without judging it.

Instruct participants to find a quiet place in the room and while they are by themselves, ask them to quietly read their journal entry aloud while they focus on the thoughts and ideas they expressed in their writing.

If time permits, conclude the exercise by asking if there are any participants who would like to volunteer to read their entry aloud to the entire group.

VARIATIONS

- Provide opportunities for participants to record their entries into a tape recorder and play them back for feedback and clarification.

- Suggest that participants record their entries into a tape recorder at home and then listen to their entries in a nonjudgmental, open fashion.

- At the end of a training session, structure a journal writing experience by asking participants to think about and then write answers to the following sentence fragments:

This period of learning has been like a . . .

This session really began for me when . . .

Particular events that stand out about this session are . . .

Angers, satisfactions, and involvements I remember about this session are . . .

Inspirations, dreams, or ideas I had during this session were . . .

Good and bad luck that happened to me during this session were . . .

Activities that have been important to me in this session are . . .

Beliefs, attitudes, or values that were called into question were . . .

Things I have avoided saying during this session are . . .

Things I want to forgive myself or others for during this session are . . .

EYES OF A FISH

*In this exercise, participants learn
to brainstorm effectively by looking
at a problem from another point of view.*

GOALS
To look at a learning problem while deferring judgment.
To experience a nonjudgmental learning process.

GROUP SIZE
Unlimited.

TIME
15–30 minutes.

MATERIALS
One 3 x 5 card for each group of four to eight participants. On each card, write the name of a being: tiger, elephant, ostrich, guppy, homeless person, CEO, etc.

*Prior to the workshop, select one or more challenging problems
for brainstorming.*

PROCESS

Introduce the exercise goals to the group and give a chalktalk on brainstorming:

▲ Brainstorming is one of the most useful creative learning methods. Brainstorming is useful for problem-solving and for learning new insights. It has been misunderstood, however, because the name has become synonymous with producing a single idea or solution.

▲ Groups of four to eight persons can quickly learn to manufacture up to fifty ideas in 5–10 minutes.

▲ The originator of the term, Alex Osborn, says the following four requirements must be met in order for a process to be considered brainstorming:

Defer judgment.

Free wheel and hang loose.

Tag on. Don't wait for an idea to come to mind, make up one out of the last one given.

Don't hold back. Call out your idea as soon as you think of it. Quantity is valued over quality.

Form groups of four to eight persons and distribute a 3 x 5 card to each group. Provide the following instructions:

▲ The problem for which you are to brainstorm solutions is **(state one of the problems that participants will be addressing in the workshop).**

▲ Select one person to be the recorder in your group to write down the ideas the rest of the group generates.

- Woodrow Wilson said: "Originality is simply a fresh pair of eyes."

- To help you discover unusual and creative ideas, you will consider the problem through the eyes of the person or creature written on the 3 x 5 card I gave your group.

- Ask a second person to repeat this phrase: "Give me another way a fish (bird, elephant, etc.) might look at this problem." You will have 5–10 minutes for this process.

After time is called, ask each group to share their findings with the larger group. Lead a closing discussion on how participants might use brainstorming to generate solutions for other problems.

YOUR PERSONAL LEARNING CONSULTANT

*Participants choose a personal learning consultant
to help them develop solutions to specific problems.*

GOALS

To learn a preventive tool for heading off learning problems.
To step out of traditional thinking methods and call in an imaginary expert.

GROUP SIZE

Unlimited.

TIME

10–30 minutes.

MATERIALS

One 3 x 5 card for each participant: on each card, write a learning
problem that relates to the session; container for cards.

PROCESS

▦ Introduce the exercise to participants using the following chalktalk:

  ▲ Calling in an expert consultant can be expensive, but you use your mind to call in an imaginary one.

  ▲ When your ideas seem to circle you back to the same answers, call in an imaginary expert consultant.

  ▲ You can often prevent problems by calling in an imaginary consultant when you begin to explore an issue.

▦ After the chalktalk is completed, give participants the following instructions:

  ▲ Select a 3 x 5 card from the pile. Close your eyes and think about the problem, then place the card and its problem in a box in your mind.

  ▲ As you are thinking about the problem, call in a consultant, who you think might help you with the problem. Anyone, living or dead, real or fictional, available or not, can be pictured in your mind—at no charge. Just call that person into your mind!

  ▲ When you have your consultant clearly in mind, ask that person "How would you solve this problem?"

▦ Have participants share what they learned from their imaginary consultant(s) with the entire group.

VARIATIONS

▦ Ask participants to list as many possible consultants for their learning problem.

■ After one imaginary consultant has been consulted, have participants ask another imaginary consultant and then compare their answers.

YOUR CHOICE

*Participants experiment with many
ways to reach a learning goal.*

GOALS
To practice novel ways for reaching learning objectives.
To discover alternate routes to learning.

GROUP SIZE
Seven small groups, each with 2–10 participants, will be formed for
this activity.

TIME
40–60 minutes.

MATERIALS
Photocopies of the **Learning Process** worksheets, one for each
small group; paper; pens or pencils; easel paper; markers.

> *Prior to the workshop, select one of your learning objectives that
> could be met effectively through a variety of techniques.*

PROCESS

■ Introduce the many ways of learning by making some of the following comments:

▲ When people set out to learn something new, they often begin—and end—by using just a few techniques, such as reading and listening.

▲ There are actually many ways of learning, and we learn more effectively when we use a variety of approaches.

▲ I have selected one of the learning objectives for this workshop (**state the objective you selected and write it on the easel paper**).

▲ You could listen to me lecture about this material, or you could read about it in a book or journal article. But we each hear and read so much every day, there's a tendency for information that comes in these ways to have little impact.

▲ Today, working in small groups, we're going to develop seven different approaches to reaching our learning objective. These approaches will be based on the seven ways of knowing described by Dr. Howard Gardner and Dr. David Lazear.

■ Form seven or more small groups and distribute one of the **Learning Process** worksheets along with paper, pens or pencils, easel paper, and markers to each group. Give the following instruction:

▲ On your worksheet, you will find one of the ways in which people learn described briefly. You will have 30 minutes to develop a process for reaching our learning objective that appeals to that way of learning. Work it out; try it out; then summarize it on the easel paper.

As participants work together, circulate among the groups to provide support.

After 30 minutes, reconvene the group.

If there is enough time, allow members of each group to present the learning process they developed, then use it to actually teach the learning objective.

If time is short, post the summaries and refer to them and the worksheets as part of a closing discussion on the benefits of multiple ways of learning.

This exercise is based on the work of Dr. David Lazear, author of Seven Ways of Knowing *(Palatine, Ill.:IRI/Skylight Publishing, 1991). To give groups other opportunities to explore their seven intelligences, see* Structured Exercises in Wellness Promotion, vol. 5, *Nancy Loving Tubesing, EdD, and Sandy Stewart Christian, MSW, eds. (Duluth, Minn.: Whole Person Associates, 1995).*

©1997 Carolyn Chambers Clark · Whole Person Associates · 210 West Michigan · Duluth, MN 55802 · (800) 247-6789

Verbal/Linguistic

Reading and listening to factual material provides our most common way to learn. For the purpose of this exercise, develop a less familiar way to learn through language. Poetry, for example, can help people capture the essence of a learning situation. By using potent images and appealing to the emotions, poetry can be far more powerful than prose.

▲ Design a process that uses poetry to reach our learning objective. Take notes on this worksheet as you make your plan.

▲ Try out the process within your group to be sure that it works the way you anticipated.

▲ When you are satisfied with the process, write a summary and brief instructions on your easel paper.

©1997 Carolyn Chambers Clark   Whole Person Associates   •   210 West Michigan   •   Duluth, MN 55802   •   (800) 247-6789

Logical/Mathematical

People often call upon logic to help them solve problems. Informally using the scientific method, they propose a solution, then accumulate evidence for and against that solution. They look for relationships and for connections.

▲ Design a process that uses scientific method to reach our learning objective. Take notes on this worksheet as you make your plan.

▲ Try out the process within your group to be sure that it works the way you anticipated.

▲ When you are satisfied with the process, write a summary and brief instructions on your easel paper.

Visual/Spatial

People who work mainly with words often find that being forced to work with images gives them a new perspective on any problem. Painting, drawing, sculpture, and architecture are visual, so also are the intriguing processes of map-making and game design.

- Design a process that uses map-making or game design to reach our learning objective. Take notes on this worksheet as you make your plan.

- Try out the process within your group to be sure that it works the way you anticipated.

- When you are satisfied with the process, write a summary and brief instructions on your easel paper.

Creating a Climate for Power Learning

©1997 Carolyn Chambers Clark · Whole Person Associates · 210 West Michigan · Duluth, MN 55802 · (800) 247-6789

Body/Kinesthetic

Chances are you have forgotten many details that you learned as a child. New information may seem to push old information right out of your mind. But if you learned to ride a bike, even if you haven't ridden for twenty years, you could probably hop on and ride away today with little trouble. We can take advantage of our kinesthetic memory by learning through movement.

▲ Design a process that uses body movement to reach our learning objective. Take notes on this worksheet as you make your plan.

▲ Try out the process within your group to be sure that it works the way you anticipated.

▲ When you are satisfied with the process, write a summary and brief instructions on your easel paper.

Musical/Rhythmic

How much poetry or prose can you recite from memory? How many songs can you sing? Most people can sing at least the first verse or chorus of a hundred or more songs. The melody and rhythm fixes the words as well as the music in their minds. Complex information and long lists, when set to music, are easily learned and long remembered.

- Design a process that uses music to reach our learning objective. Take notes on this worksheet as you make your plan.

- Try out the process within your group to be sure that it works the way you anticipated.

- When you are satisfied with the process, write a summary and brief instructions on your easel paper.

©1997 Carolyn Chambers Clark Whole Person Associates • 210 West Michigan • Duluth, MN 55802 • (800) 247-6789

Creating a Climate for Power Learning

©1997 Carolyn Chambers Clark Whole Person Associates • 210 West Michigan • Duluth, MN 55802 • (800) 247-6789

Interpersonal

Working together, we learn from each other. By analyzing and discussing a problem, we share our ideas, but by role-playing that same problem, we share even more, gaining empathy for all those affected by the problem.

▲ Design a process that uses role-playing or simulation to reach our learning objective. Take notes on this worksheet as you make your plan.

▲ Try out the process within your group to be sure that it works the way you anticipated.

▲ When you are satisfied with the process, write a summary and brief instructions on your easel paper.

©1997 Carolyn Chambers Clark Whole Person Associates • 210 West Michigan • Duluth, MN 55802 • (800) 247-6789

Intrapersonal

When we attempt to solve a problem, we most often look outside ourselves for information or advice. Rarely do we have the confidence to trust our inner resources. A guided meditation can help people quiet their minds and tap their own accumulated wisdom.

- Design a process that uses guided meditation to reach our learning objective. Take notes on this worksheet as you make your plan.

- Try out the process within your group to be sure that it works the way you anticipated.

- When you are satisfied with the process, write a summary and brief instructions on your easel paper.

Creating a Climate for Power Learning

IF I WERE . . .

*Participants practice ways to
release themselves from fear
of meeting their learning goals.*

GOALS
To use creative imagination to empathize with someone else's plight.
To extend what is learned from the work setting.

GROUP SIZE
Unlimited.

TIME
10–30 minutes.

MATERIALS
One 3 x 5 card for each participant. On each card, write a difficult
situation for participants to role-play: Your boss has to fire you;
Your mother visits you in prison; Your worst enemy is in trouble;
Your child must confess to misbehavior, etc.

PROCESS

▪ Introduce the concept of empathy to participants—the skill of understanding what it's like to walk in someone else's shoes without actually going through the experience—then provide the following instructions:

  ▴ I am going to pass around a pack of cards to the group. I would like each person to select a card, then find a partner.

  ▴ Each card contains a different life situation for you to act out with your partner. These situations are challenging and stressful.

  ▴ You will have 2 minutes to talk with your partner about what it must be like to be in the situation posed on one of your cards. In your conversation, try to develop empathy for the people described on your card. I will let you know when 2 minutes are up.

▪ After 2 minutes, give the following instruction:

  ▴ You will now have 3 minutes to role-play the situation with each other. Begin by deciding which role each of you will play.

▪ After 3 minutes are up and everyone is finished with their role play, proceed with the following instructions:

  ▴ Switch your focus to your partner's situation card. You will have 2 minutes to discuss the situation. I will call time when 2 minutes are up.

▪ After 2 minutes, instruct participants to act out the situation on their second card.

▪ When everyone is finished with their second role play, reconvene the entire group and lead a closing discussion by asking the following questions:

▲ What did you learn from playing out the chosen situations?

▲ How can you use the process you learned in these role plays to help you be more empathetic?

FOOD FOR THOUGHT

Participants use an imagery exercise to help them visualize the process of learning new information.

GOAL
To experience a situation analogous to learning.

GROUP SIZE
Unlimited.

TIME
15 minutes.

MATERIALS
One orange, apple, or banana for each participant.

PROCESS
Introduce the goal of the exercise and provide the following instructions:

    ▲ I am going to pass a bowl of fruit around the group, and I would like each of you to take one piece. Just as this fruit is food for your body, new learning is food for your mind. Let's take a few minutes to experience this analogy.

▲ Sniff your piece of fruit. The smell may already be making you hungry. Opening a book or entering a training session can similarly make you hungry or eager for the learning experience.

▲ Take a bite of your fruit, savoring the delicious taste, letting it roll around in your mouth. Learning something new is exciting and tantalizing, full of almost indescribable sensations.

▲ As you finish chewing your mouthful of fruit, swallow and picture the fruit taking a long trip down the digestive track, entering the stomach, moving into the intestines where it is further digested and becomes part of the body or is expelled as waste. When you digest new information, what is useful is remembered and becomes part of you. What is not considered useful you will forget or discard.

▨ While participants finish eating their piece of fruit, suggest to them that any new information can be thought of as food for their minds.

ESCAPING FROM HABIT

Participants draw a picture of themselves escaping from the snares that habit has placed out for them.

GOALS
To depict learning habits.
To discuss ways to escape from stumbling blocks to learning.

GROUP SIZE
Unlimited.

TIME
10–30 minutes.

MATERIALS
Drawing paper; crayons or colored marking pens; easel pad and markers.

PROCESS
▪ Introduce the exercise to the group with a few comments on learning difficulties:

Creating a Climate for Power Learning

- At times, each of us can find it difficult to concentrate on learning tasks.

- You may experience those difficulties as snares that capture and hold you fast, as roadblocks too high to climb over, or in some other way.

- One way to be successful at learning is to visualize yourself conquering these blocks.

Distribute paper and crayons or marking pens, then give the following instructions:

- Using the materials I gave you, draw yourself successfully confronting whatever tends to block your learning.

- Use pictures, symbols, or words.

After 10 minutes, call time and lead a closing discussion using the following questions:

- What kinds of snares, blocks, and sidetrips are interfering with your learning?

  Ask the group to call them out so you or a volunteer can list them on the easel pad.

- What ways have you found to successfully confront and conquer these problems?

- How can you use what you have learned in this activity in future learning situations?

PROJECT YOURSELF INTO TOMORROW

Participants are guided through an imagery exercise to focus on what they will be like tomorrow after they have learned the information from this training session.

GOALS
To use imagery skills to provide incentives for learning.
To project themselves into the future.

GROUP SIZE
Unlimited.

TIME
10–20 minutes.

MATERIALS
None.

PROCESS

This exercise is often used as a final learning experience at the end of a training session, but can be used when participants are feeling frustrated or need to renew their interest in the learning objectives.

▨ Ask participants to get comfortable in their chairs and close their eyes.

▨ Read aloud the following script or devise one of your own to help participants imagine what they'll be like tomorrow after this learning session. Go slowly, pausing briefly at each ellipses:

Feel the warmth and comfort of your bed . . .
picture yourself thinking about this learning session
and having positive thoughts about what happened
here today . . .
how pleasant it was . . .
how much you learned . . .

Mentally list all the things you learned . . .
about the topic . . . and about yourself . . .
all the things you want to apply to your life . . .

Write them all down on a mental blackboard in your mind . . .
perhaps using green chalk for the information you learned . . .
using red chalk for the things you learned about yourself . . .

Picture yourself getting ready for work and feeling confident that you can apply everything you learned . . .

Visualize yourself leaving the house and heading for work . . .
feeling so glad you learned everything you did yesterday . . .
feeling really eager to get to work and use what you learned . . .

Picture yourself getting to work and having a very positive attitude about going back to your work site . . .

feeling more confident, positive, and eager
than you have in a long time . . .

Picture your boss responding very positively to you
as you begin to apply what you learned yesterday . . .
picture your peers responding very positively
as you show them your new skills . . .
picture them asking you to teach them these skills . . .
some of the things you learned . . .

There may be one person, or a few
who don't respond positively . . .
but you find yourself still remaining confident . . .
knowing that it doesn't matter what other people
think about your new skills . . .
you will find a way to use them for your benefit . . .
you will find a way to remain positive and confident . . .

Now, get ready to open your eyes . . .
but, before you do . . .
bask in those positive, warm feelings
about what you learned . . .
remember you can keep those feelings
as long as you want to . . .
and even if they begin to fade . . .
you can get them back again
merely by picturing yourself in this training session
at a time when you felt positive and confident . . .

Now, gradually open your eyes . . .
feeling positive, confident, and self-assured, . . .
ready to leave this session, taking with you all the positive,
confident, and self-assured feelings you experienced here.

Creating a Climate for Power Learning

■ After participants open their eyes, lead a closing discussion by asking them to share insights they gained during the imagery sequence.

I'M CREATIVE

*By writing or drawing with their nondominant hands,
participants tap into the right side of their brain
to release creative thoughts and reactions.*

GOALS
To tap into the right side of the brain and release creative thoughts
and reactions.
To share with peers what was learned from using the nondominant
hand.

GROUP SIZE
Unlimited.

TIME
15–30 minutes.

MATERIALS
Blank paper; pens or pencils.

PROCESS
Introduce the exercise to participants as a process designed to

encourage openness and creativity. Distribute paper and pens or pencils to everyone.

■ Ask participants to write or draw responses to the following questions using their dominant hand, the one they usually write with. They will have 2 minutes for each question. They should not censor their responses, but write the first thing that comes to their mind.

▲ What do I hope to learn in this session?

▲ What worries do I have about this session?

▲ What can I do to make sure I learn as much as possible for the rest of this session?

■ When everyone has finished answering these questions, continue with the following comment and instructions:

▲ When we write with our nondominant hand, it taps into the creative holistic side of the brain. If we are open to the experience, we may get some interesting responses to the same three questions we previously answered.

▲ To explore this issue, I would like everyone to use their nondominant hand this time and write or draw answers to the same three questions. Write the first thing that comes to your mind. Do not be critical or judgmental of your ideas or the way they look on paper.

Repeat for the group the three questions listed above.

■ When everyone has finished writing, lead a closing discussion using the following questions:

▲ What feelings did you experience when you wrote answers to the questions with your dominant hand?

- What feelings did you experience when you wrote with your nondominant hand?

- What differences or similarities did you notice in your responses to the questions when you wrote with different hands?

- How can you use nondominant writing in the future to expand your ways of experiencing, understanding, and learning from a situation?

WHOLE PERSON ASSOCIATES RESOURCES

All printed, audio, and video resources developed by Whole Person Associates are designed to address the whole person—physical, emotional, mental, spiritual, and social. On the next pages, trainers will find a wide array of resources that offer ready-to-use ideas and concepts they can add to their programs.

SELF-HELP RESOURCES

OVERCOMING PANIC, ANXIETY, & PHOBIAS
Shirley Babior, LCSW, MFCC, and Carol Goldman, LICSW

This practical self-help guide provides concrete advice as well as hopeful personal stories of recovery. Tips include managing catastrophic thoughts with rational responses, facing fearful situations, dealing with setbacks, and using relaxation to reduce physical symptoms.

❑ **Overcoming Panic, Anxiety, & Phobias / $12.95**

DON'T GET MAD, GET FUNNY!
Leigh Anne Jasheway, Illustrations by Geoffrey Welles

Jasheway guides readers through identifying the seven symptoms of stress, surveying your current stress level, creating a stress management plan, determining the types of things you find humorous, and learning five simple steps to put more humor in your life.

❑ **Don't Get Mad, Get Funny! / $12.95**

SLEEP SECRETS FOR SHIFT WORKERS & PEOPLE WITH OFF-BEAT SCHEDULES
David Morgan

Twenty-five million people in the United States work shifts, and half of them report sleep problems. *Sleep Secrets*—the first book to address the unique problems shift workers face—helps people improve the quality of their sleep so they can lead happier, healthier, more productive lives.

❑ **Sleep Secrets / $12.95**

WORKSHOPS-IN-A-BOOK

KICKING YOUR STRESS HABITS
A Do-It-Yourself Guide for Coping with Stress
Donald A. Tubesing, PhD

This workshop-in-a-book actively involves the reader in assessing stressful patterns and developing more effective coping strategies. The 10-step planning process and 20 skills for managing stress make *Kicking Your Stress Habits* an ideal text for stress management classes in many different settings, from hospitals to universities.

❑ **Kicking Your Stress Habits / $15.95**

SEEKING YOUR HEALTHY BALANCE
A Do-It-Yourself Guide to Whole Person Well-Being
Donald A. Tubesing, PhD, and Nancy Loving Tubesing, EdD

Seeking Your Healthy Balance helps readers discover how to develop a more balanced lifestyle by learning effective ways to juggle work, self, and others; by clarifying self-care options; and by discovering and setting their own personal priorities.

❑ **Seeking Your Healthy Balance / $15.95**

ADDITIONAL TRAINERS RESOURCES

MIND-BODY MAGIC
Martha Belknap, MA

Make any presentation more powerful with one of these 40 feel-good activities. Handy tips with each activity show you how to use it in your presentation, plus ideas for enhancing or extending the activity, and suggestions for adapting it for your teaching goals and audience. Use *Mind-Body Magic* to present any topic with pizzazz!

- ❑ **Mind-Body Magic / $21.95**
- ❑ **Worksheet Masters/ $9.95**

INSTANT ICEBREAKERS
50 Powerful Catalysts for Group Interaction and High-Impact Learning
Sandy Stewart Christian, MSW, and
Nancy Loving Tubesing, EdD, Editors

Introduce the subject at hand and introduce participants to each other with these proven strategies that apply to all kinds of audiences and appeal to many learning styles.

Step-by-step instructions and dazzling graphics on the worksheets make any presentation a breeze.

- ❑ **Instant Icebreakers / $24.95**
- ❑ **Worksheet Masters / $9.95**

PLAYING ALONG
37 Group Learning Activities Borrowed from Improvisational Theater
Izzy Gesell, MS

Set the stage for learning and growth with these innovative, playful activities borrowed from a classic art form: improvisational theater. Whatever your topic, these brief (5–10 minute) exercises activate the all-important learning skills of listening, accepting, affirming, imagining, and trusting—and pave the way for personal growth or organizational change.

- ❑ **Playing Along / $21.95**

PLAYFUL ACTIVITIES FOR POWERFUL PRESENTATIONS
Bruce Williamson

Spice up presentations with healthy laughter. The 40 creative energizers in *Playful Activities for Powerful Presentations* will enhance learning, stimulate communication, promote teamwork, and reduce resistance to group interaction.

- ❑ **Playful Activities for Powerful Presentations / $21.95**

To order: call 1-800-247-6789

ADDITIONAL GROUP PROCESS RESOURCES

WORKING WITH WOMEN'S GROUPS, Volumes 1 & 2
Louise Yolton Eberhardt

When leading a women's group, don't just rely on personal experience and intuition—equip yourself with these volumes of proven exercises. Louise Yolton Eberhardt has distilled more than a quarter century of experience into nearly a hundred processes addressing the issues that are most important to women today.

The two volumes of *Working with Women's Groups* have been completely revised and updated. *Volume 1* explores consciousness raising, self-discovery, and assertiveness training. *Volume 2* looks at sexuality issues, women of color, and leadership skills training.

❏ **Working with Women's Groups, Vols 1 & 2 / $24.95 each**
❏ **Worksheet Masters, Vols 1 & 2 / $9.95 each**

WORKING WITH MEN'S GROUPS
Roger Karsk and Bill Thomas

Working with Men's Groups has been updated to reflect the reality of men's lives in the 1990s. Each exercise follows a structured pattern to help trainers develop either onetime workshops or ongoing groups that explore men's issues in four key areas: self-discovery, consciousness raising, intimacy, and parenting.

❏ **Working with Men's Groups / $24.95**
❏ **Worksheet Masters / $9.95**

WELLNESS ACTIVITIES FOR YOUTH, Volumes 1 & 2
Sandy Queen

Each volume of *Wellness Activities for Youth* provides 36 complete classroom activities that help leaders teach children and teenagers about wellness with a whole person approach and an emphasis on FUN. The concepts include: values, stress and coping, self-esteem, personal well-being, and social wellness.

Curriculum developer Sandy Queen designed these whole-person, "no-put-down" activities for kids from middle school to high school age, but many can be adapted for families or even for the corporate setting.

❏ **Wellness Activities for Youth, Vols 1 & 2 / $21.95 each**
❏ **Worksheet Masters, Vols 1 & 2 / $9.95 each**

To order: call 1-800-247-6789

TOPICAL GROUP RESOURCES

WORKING WITH GROUPS ON SPIRITUAL THEMES
Elaine Hopkins, Zo Woods, Russell Kelley, Katrina Bentley,
and James Murphy

True wellness must address the spirit. Many groups that
originally form around issues such as physical or mental
health, stress management, or relationships eventually
recognize the importance of spiritual issues. The material
contained in this manual helps health professionals initiate discussion
on spiritual needs in a logical, organized fashion that induces a high
level of comfort for group members and leaders.

❑ **Working with Groups on Spiritual Themes / $24.95**
❑ **Worksheet Masters / $9.95**

WORKING WITH GROUPS TO OVERCOME
PANIC, ANXIETY, & PHOBIAS
Shirley Babior, LCSW, MFCC, and Carol Goldman, LICSW

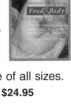

Written especially for therapists, this manual presents well-
researched, state-of-the-art treatment strategies for a
variety of anxiety disorders. It includes treatment goals,
basic anxiety-recovery exercises, and recovery enhancers
that encourage lifestyle changes. Sessions in this manual are related
directly to the chapters in *Overcoming Panic, Anxiety, & Phobias.*

❑ **Working with Groups to Overcome Panic, Anxiety, & Phobias / $24.95**
❑ **Worksheet Masters / $9.95**

WORKING WITH GROUPS TO EXPLORE
FOOD & BODY CONNECTIONS
Sandy Stewart Christian, MSW, Editor

This collection of 36 group processes gathered from experts
around the country tackles complex and painful issues nearly
everyone is concerned about—dieting, weight, healthy
eating, fitness, body image, and self-esteem—using a whole
person approach that advocates health and fitness for people of all sizes.

❑ **Working with Groups to Explore Food & Body Connections / $24.95**
❑ **Worksheet Masters / $9.95**

CREATIVE PLANNING FOR THE SECOND HALF OF LIFE
Burton Kreitlow, PhD, and Doris Kreitlow, MS

This is the first book to help group leaders design a
presentation or workshop that addresses the whole-person
needs of people ages 50 and up. These 29 structured
exercises explore ways of planning for retirement by finding
intriguing ways to make a useful life for yourself—not
simply setting aside money for the day you quit working.

❑ **Creative Planning for the Second Half of Life / $24.95**
❑ **Worksheet Masters / $9.95**

To order: call 1-800-247-6789

WORKING WITH GROUPS FROM DYSFUNCTIONAL FAMILIES
Cheryl Hetherington

This collection of 29 proven group activities is designed to heal the pain that results from living in a dysfunctional family. With these exercises leaders can promote healing, build self-esteem, encourage sharing, and help participants acknowledge their feelings.

❑ **Working with Groups from Dysfunctional Families / $24.95**
❑ **Worksheet Masters / $9.95**

WORKING WITH GROUPS ON FAMILY ISSUES
Sandy Stewart Christian, MSW, LICSW

These 24 structured exercises combine the knowledge of marriage and family experts with practical techniques to help you move individuals, couples, and families toward positive change. Topics include divorce, single parenting, stepfamilies, gay and lesbian relationships, working partners, and more.

❑ **Working with Groups on Family Issues / $24.95**
❑ **Worksheet Masters / $9.95**

WORKING WITH GROUPS IN THE WORKPLACE

BRIDGING THE GENDER GAP
Louise Yolton Eberhardt

Bridging the Gender Gap contains a wealth of exercises for trainers to use in gender role awareness groups, diversity training, couples workshops, college classes, and youth seminars.

❑ **Bridging the Gender Gap / $24.95**
❑ **Worksheet Masters / $9.95**

CONFRONTING SEXUAL HARASSMENT
Louise Yolton Eberhardt

Confronting Sexual Harassment presents exercises that trainers can safely use with groups to constructively explore the issues of sexual harassment, look at the underlying causes, understand the law, motivate men to become allies, and empower women to speak up.

❑ **Confronting Sexual Harassment / $24.95**
❑ **Worksheet Masters / $9.95**

CELEBRATING DIVERSITY
Cheryl Hetherington

Celebrating Diversity helps people confront and question the beliefs, prejudices, and fears that can separate them from others. Carefully written exercises help trainers present these sensitive issues in the workplace as well as in educational settings.

❑ **Celebrating Diversity / $24.95**
❑ **Worksheet Masters / $9.95**

To order: call 1-800-247-6789

STRESS AND WELLNESS RESOURCES

STRUCTURED EXERCISES IN STRESS MANAGEMENT, VOLS 1–5
STRUCTURED EXERCISES IN WELLNESS PROMOTION, VOLS 1–5
Nancy Loving Tubesing, EdD, Donald A. Tubesing, PhD,
and Sandy Stewart Christian, MSW, Editors

Each book in these two series contains 36 ready-to-use experiential learning activities, focusing on whole person health (body, mind, spirit, emotions, relationships, and lifestyle) or effective stress management.

Developed by an interdisciplinary team of leaders in the wellness movement nationwide and top stress management professionals, these exercises actively encourage participants to examine their current attitudes and patterns. All process designs are clearly explained and have been thoroughly field-tested with diverse audiences so that trainers can use them with confidence.

Each volume brims with practical ideas that mix and match, allowing trainers to develop new programs for varied settings, audiences, and time frames. Each volume contains **Icebreakers, Action Planners, Closing Processes,** and **Group Energizers**. The *Wellness Promotion* volumes also include **Wellness Explorations** and **Self-Care Strategies.** The *Stress Management* volumes include **Stress Assessments, Management Strategies,** and **Skill Builders.**

❑ **Stress or Wellness 8 1/2" x 11" Loose-leaf Edition—Vols 1–5 / $54.95 each****
❑ **Stress or Wellness 6" x 9" Softcover Edition—Vols 1–5 / $29.95 each**
❑ **Worksheet Masters—Vols 1–5 / $9.95 each**
    ** Worksheet Masters are included as part of the loose-leaf edition.**

STRESS AND WELLNESS REFERENCE GUIDE
A Comprehensive Index to the Chalktalks, Processes, and Activities in the Whole Person Structured Exercises Series
Nancy Loving Tubesing, EdD, Editor

This handy index is your key to over 360 teaching designs in the ten-volume *Structured Exercises in Stress and Wellness* series—organized by theme, time frame, level of self-disclosure, trainer experience level, and goals. This book includes all ten Tips for Trainers sections, with workshop outlines and suggestions especially for the workplace.

The *Stress and Wellness Reference Guide* makes it easy to plan a workshop by mixing and matching exercises suitable to your audience. You'll find easy-to-read charts with a quick view of group processes and activities—so you can find your favorites to use with any group.

❑ **Stress and Wellness Reference Guide / $29.95**

To order: call 1-800-247-6789

RELAXATION AUDIOTAPES

SENSATIONAL RELAXATION—$11.95 each

When stress piles up, it becomes a heavy load both physically and emotionally. These full-length relaxation experiences will teach you techniques that can be used whenever you feel that stress is getting out of control. Choose one you like and repeat it daily until it becomes second nature, then recall that technique whenever you need it or try a new one every day.

- ❑ **Countdown to Relaxation /** Countdown 19:00, Staircase 19:00
- ❑ **Daybreak / Sundown /** Daybreak 22:00, Sundown 22:00
- ❑ **Take a Deep Breath /** Breathing for Relaxation 17:00, Magic Ball 17:00
- ❑ **Relax . . . Let Go . . . Relax /** Revitalization 27:00, Relaxation 28:00
- ❑ **StressRelease /** Quick Tension Relievers 22:00, Progressive Relaxation 20:00
- ❑ **Warm and Heavy /** Warm 24:00, Heavy 23:00

STRESS BREAKS—$11.95 each

Do you need a short energy booster or a quick stress reliever? If you don't know what type of relaxation you like, or if you are new to guided relaxation techniques, try one of our **Stress Breaks** for a quick refocusing or change of pace any time of the day.

- ❑ **BreakTime /** Solar Power 8:00, Belly Breathing 9:00, Fortune Cookie 9:00, Mother Earth 11:00, Big Yawn 5:00, Affirmation 11:00
- ❑ **Natural Tranquilizers /** Clear the Deck 10:00, Body Scan 10:00, 99 Countdown 10:00, Calm Down 9:00, Soothing Colors 11:00, Breathe Ten 9:00
- ❑ **Stress Escapes /** Sensory Relaxation 18:00, Breathing Meditation 11:00, Anchoring 12:00, Breathe Away Tension 8:00, Moans and Groans 9:00
- ❑ **Worry Stoppers /** 10-Second Breathing 5:00, Trouble Bubbles 5:45, Train of Thought 5:30, Rest in Peace 6:00, Passive Progressive Relaxation 22:00

DO-IT-YOURSELF RELAXATION—$11.95 each

Learn the basics of specialized techniques you can use whenever you need them to trigger your body's relaxation response.

- ❑ **Yoga /** Cleansing Breath 6:30, Good Morning World 11:00, Relaxation Pose 10:30, Complete and Humming Breath 9:00, Cobra 10:00, Seaweed and Oak 9:00
- ❑ **Massage /** Pushing My Buttons 18:00, All Ears 5:00, Fingertip Face Massage 15:00, Eye Soothers 7:00

DAYDREAMS—$11.95 each

Escape from the stress around you with guided tours to beautiful places. The quick escapes in our **Daydreams** tapes will lead your imagination away from your everyday cares so you can resume your tasks relaxed and comforted.

- ❑ **Daydreams 1: Getaways /** Cabin Retreat 11:00, Night Sky 10:00, Hot Spring 7:00, Mountain View 8:00, Superior Sail 8:00
- ❑ **Daydreams 2: Peaceful Places /** Ocean Tides 11:00, City Park 10:00, Hammock 8:00, Meadow 11:00
- ❑ **Daydreams 3: Relaxing Retreats /** Melting Candle 5:00, Tropical Paradise 10:00, Sanctuary 7:00, Floating Clouds 5:00, Seasons 9:00, Beach Tides 9:00

To order: call 1-800-247-6789

GUIDED MEDITATION—$11.95 each
Take a step beyond relaxation. The imagery in our full-length meditations will help you discover your strengths, find healing, make positive life changes, and recognize your inner wisdom.

- ❏ **Inner Healing** / Inner Healing 20:00, Peace with Pain 20:00
- ❏ **Personal Empowering** / My Gifts 22:00, Hidden Strengths 21:00
- ❏ **Healthy Balancing** / Inner Harmony 20:00, Regaining Equilibrium 20:00
- ❏ **Spiritual Centering** / Spiritual Centering 20:00 (male and female narration)
- ❏ **Mantras** / Illumination 23:00, Transformation 23:00

WILDERNESS DAYDREAMS—$11.95 each
Discover the healing power of nature with the four tapes in our **Wilderness Daydreams** series. The eight special journeys will transport you from your harried, stressful surroundings to the peaceful serenity of words and water.

- ❏ **Canoe / Rain /** Canoe 19:00, Rain 22:00
- ❏ **Island / Spring /** Island 19:00, Spring 19:00
- ❏ **Campfire / Stream /** Campfire 17:00, Stream 19:00
- ❏ **Sailboat / Pond /** Sailboat 25:00, Pond 25:00

MINI-MEDITATIONS—$11.95 each
These brief guided visualizations begin by focusing your breathing and uncluttering your mind so that you can concentrate on a sequence of sensory images that promote relaxation, centering, healing, growth, and spiritual awareness.

- ❏ **Healing Visions /** Rocking Chair 5:00, Pine Forest 8:00, Long Lost Confidant 10:00, Caterpillar to Butterfly 7:00, Superpowers 9:00, Tornado 8:00
- ❏ **Refreshing Journeys /** 1 to 10 10:00, Thoughts Library 11:00, Visualizing Change 6:00, Magic Carpet 9:00, Pond of Love 9:00, Cruise 9:00
- ❏ **Healthy Choices /** Lifestyle 7:15, Eating 7:30, Exercise 7:15, Stress 7:30, Relationships 7:00, Change 7:30

DO-IT-YOURSELF WELLNESS
Make mind/body self-care breaks an integral part of your wellness lifestyle with these affirming breathing and imagery routines for special needs.

- ❏ **Eating /** Mealtime Meditation 13:00, Filling Your Empty Spaces 15:00, Mood Surfing 11:00, Hungers 17:00
- ❏ **Body Image /** Relaxing Breath 5:45, Body Sensing 14:15, Body Talk 12:00, Cleansing Breath Relaxation 5:45, Eyes of Love 26:15
- ❏ **Calm Down /** Progressive Relaxation 25:00, Calming Breath—Peaceful Pool 14:00, Mindful Meditation 11:00

MUSIC ONLY—$11.95 each
No relaxation program would be complete without relaxing melodies to play as background for a prepared script or to enjoy favorite techniques on your own. Steven Eckels composed his melodies specifically for relaxation. These "musical prayers for healing" will calm your body, mind, and spirit.

- ❏ **Tranquility /** Awakening 20:00, Repose 20:00
- ❏ **Harmony /** Waves of Light 30:00, Rising Mist 10:00, Frankincense 10:00, Angelica 10:00
- ❏ **Serenity /** Radiance 20:00, Quiescence 10:00, Evanescence 10:00

MUSIC ONLY CD—$15.95
- ❏ **Contemplation** / Mystical Meditation 31:00, Musical Mantras 31:00

To order: call 1-800-247-6789

ABOUT WHOLE PERSON ASSOCIATES

At Whole Person Associates we're 100% committed to providing stress and wellness materials that involve participants and provide a "whole person" focus—body, mind, spirit, and relationships.

ABOUT THE OWNERS

Whole Person Associates was created by the vision of two people: Donald A. Tubesing, PhD, and Nancy Loving Tubesing, EdD. Don and Nancy have been active in the stress management/wellness promotion movement for over twenty years—consulting, leading seminars, writing, and publishing. Most of our early products were the result of their creativity and expertise. Living proof that you can "stay evergreen," Don and Nancy remain the driving force behind the company and are still very active in developing new products that touch people's lives.

ABOUT THE COMPANY

Whole Person Associates was "born" in Duluth, Minnesota, and we remain committed to our lovely city on the shore of Lake Superior. We put the same high quality into every product we offer, translating the best of current research into practical, accessible, easy-to-use materials. We create the best possible resources to help our customers teach about stress management and wellness promotion. And our friendly, resourceful employees are committed to helping you find the products that fit your needs.

We also strive to treat our customers as we would like to be treated. If we fall short of our goals in any way, please let us know.

ABOUT OUR ASSOCIATES

Who are the "associates" in Whole Person Associates? They're the trainers, authors, musicians, and others who have developed much of the material you see on these pages. We're always on the lookout for high-quality products that reflect our "whole person" philosophy and fill a need for our customers. Our products were developed by experts who are at the top of their fields, and we're very proud to be associated with them.

ABOUT OUR CUSTOMERS

We'd love to hear from you! Let us know what you think of our products—how you use them in your work, what additional products you'd like to see, and what shortcomings you've noted. Write us or call on our toll-free line. We look forward to hearing from you!

**Call 1-800-247-6789
to receive a catalog or to place an order**